SUPERSTARS of HISTORY

THE GOOD, THE BAD, and THE BRAINY

SUPERSTARS of HISTORY

THE GOOD, THE BAD, and THE BRAINY

CREATED BY BASHER ★ WRITTEN BY R.J. GRANT

SCHOLASTIC INC.

Dedicated to Claire, Kas & Leigh Coleman

ISBN 978-0-545-68024-0

Created by Basher and Toucan Books Ltd.
Text: Reg Grant
Consultant: Dr. Jacob F. Field
Art Direction: Simon Basher
Editor: Anna Southgate
Designer: Leah Germann
Proofreader: Marion Dent
Index: Marie Lorimer

12 11 10 9 8 7 6 5 4 3 2 1   14 15 16 17 18 19

Printed in China by Super Step International Ltd.
First printing, September 2014

CONTENTS

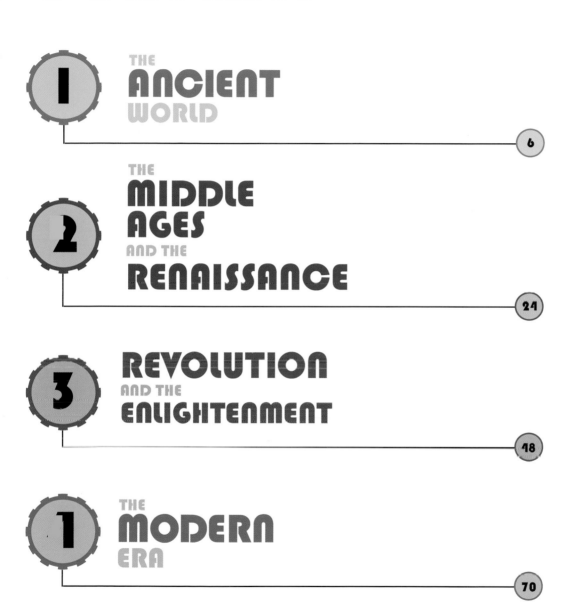

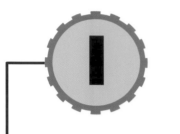

THE ANCIENT WORLD

ca. 1258 BCE

WAR AND PEACE
Ramses II signs the world's first treaty as his battle against the Hittites draws to a close.

335 BCE

SMART THINKING
Aristotle opens a school — and his mind — to a new generation of philosophers in Athens.

334 BCE

BRUTE FORCE
Alexander the Great embarks on a victorious campaign against the vast Persian Empire.

ca. 250 BCE

ROUND AND ROUND
Archimedes devises the number, "pi." Pi is used to calculate the area of a circle; it remains the standard forever.

221 BCE

CHINA UNITED
Qin Shihuangdi unifies the warring Chinese states to become First Emperor of China.

1303–1213 BCE
RAMSES II

384–322 BCE
ARISTOTLE

356–323 BCE
ALEXANDER THE GREAT

287–212 BCE
ARCHIMEDES

259–210 BCE
QIN SHIHUANGDI

Among these superstars of ancient times, you'll find a handful who liked to flex their muscles. In building vast empires of their own, these bold leaders of men and women took on mighty opponents — sometimes winning, sometimes losing — in bitter clashes. There are some great minds among these ancients, too. Archimedes may well be the greatest scientist and mathematician of his age, while Aristotle is considered one of the most influential thinkers of all time!

44 BCE
ROME RULES
Julius Caesar — master of the Roman Empire — is stabbed to death in Rome.

312 CE
FAITH IN GOD
Constantine the Great converts to Christianity, changing the face of the Roman Empire.

452 CE
BARBARIC BEHAVIOR
Attila the Hun takes on the Roman Empire, but his brutal attacks fail to bring Rome to its knees.

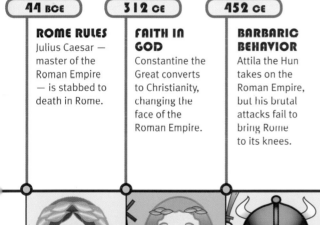

100–44 BCE
JULIUS CAESAR

272–337 CE
CONSTANTINE THE GREAT

400–454 CE
ATTILA THE HUN

"King of kings am I."

RAMSES II

I'm no shrinking violet! Born to rule mighty Egypt, I took over most of my dad's work when I was fourteen and became pharaoh before hitting thirty. I reigned for sixty-six years. Halfway through my time as pharaoh, the priests declared me a god — way to go! I boasted of having one hundred sons and sixty daughters. Don't ask me their names! I lost count of my wives, too, although Nefertari was my favorite.

My Fearsome Reputation

The most exciting moment of my life was at the Battle of Kadesh in modern-day Syria, where I fought my great enemies, the Hittites, who ruled most of modern-day Turkey. At least five thousand chariots clashed in what some claim to have been a draw. A draw? Not at all! The battle was a magnificent victory for me — I won it fair and square. In case anyone forgot how great I was, I had colossal statues of myself carved in stone, some of them sixty-five feet (twenty meters) tall. Well, we all need someone to look up to! After I died, I was mummified and buried in the Valley of the Kings at Luxor. For many years now, I have been known as "Ramses the Great," and that suits me just fine!

TIMELINE

ca. 1303 BCE Born the son of Pharaoh Seti I

ca. 1289 BCE Entrusted with a large share of his father's power

ca. 1279 BCE Becomes pharaoh

ca. 1274 BCE Fights the Battle of Kadesh against the Hittites

ca. 1213 BCE Dies and is buried in the Valley of the Kings at Luxor

LEGACY

One of the most famous ancient Egyptian pharaohs, Ramses the Great took Egypt to the peak of its power. Some of the magnificent palaces, temples, and statues that he built are still standing more than three thousand years later.

TRAVELING PHARAOH

In 1974, Ramses' mummified body was flown from Cairo's Egyptian museum to Paris, France, for inspection by experts. For the journey, the mummy had its own passport. Under "occupation" it said "King: deceased." Examination of the body showed that the pharaoh suffered from crippling arthritis and rotten teeth.

FELLOW PHARAOHS

★ **Hatshepsut** (ca. 1508–1458 BCE) was Egypt's most successful female pharaoh, ruling for more than twenty years.

★ **Akhenaten** (ca. 1380–1334 BCE) was famous for trying to convert Egyptians to a new religion. He failed.

★ **Cleopatra** (69–30 BCE) was the last pharaoh. She killed herself as the Roman Empire took over Egypt.

?

Did Ramses II build the famous pyramids?
No, but he did build the famous temples at Abu Simbel and Karnak. The pyramids date back to the Old Kingdom, over one thousand years before Ramses was born.

PEACEMAKER

Ramses was responsible for the world's first-known peace treaty, ending war with the Hittites in ca. 1258 BCE. The treaty (a type of contract) included agreements for working together to resolve any future differences without war. Today visitors to New York can find a copy of the treaty displayed in the United Nations headquarters.

"In all things of nature
there is something of the **marvelous.**"

ARISTOTLE

I was raised in ancient Greece, a philosopher in a land of philosophers. And although I lived a long time ago, some say I knew more than any other person who has ever existed — and I mean ever! Men like my teacher, Plato, and his mentor, Socrates, were real thinkers, but I understood that thinking wasn't enough. I knew that ideas could only take you so far and, to get further, you had to observe the world up close and even take it apart.

I studied dead animals in order to understand how their bodies worked. I broke open chickens' eggs to see how their chicks developed. I valued the knowledge of ordinary people and asked fishermen about fish and beekeepers about bees. Over time, I became an authority on many subjects — zoology, botany, physics, geology, meteorology, psychology, astronomy, anatomy, logic, poetry, politics, you name it.

A Fear of Knowledge
At my school, in Athens, I taught the next generation of philosophers to think. But in the end my free thinking was too radical for the city's bigwigs. I was forced to flee the city and died in exile.

TIMELINE

384 BCE Born in Stagira, Northern Greece

366 BCE Attends Plato's academy in Athens

342 BCE Becomes tutor to the future Alexander the Great

335 BCE Opens his own school, the Lyceum, in Athens

322 BCE Dies in Chalcis, on the island of Euboea

PHILOSOPHICAL GREEKS

★ **Socrates** (469–399 BCE) taught philosophy by making students think for themselves.
★ **Plato** (427–347 BCE) believed that ideas were real and the material world an illusion.
★ **Diogenes** (412–323 BCE) lived a simple life in criticism of society.
★ **Democritus** (ca. 460–370 BCE) said that matter consisted of atoms moving in an empty space.

LEGACY

Aristotle was probably the most influential thinker of all time. Despite taking another two thousand years to bear fruit, his use of observation and logic to understand the natural world formed the basis of modern science.

BIG MISTAKES

Aristotle had a great mind, but he wasn't always right. Here are some of his bloopers. He thought that:

✱ Men had more teeth than women.
✱ The brain was the body's cooling system, and all thinking took place in the heart.
✱ Flies had four legs.
✱ The Earth was the center of the universe.

LOST AND FOUND

One thousand years after his death, almost nothing was known of Aristotle's writings. Then, in the Middle Ages, scholars began translating fragments of old Greek texts into Arabic and Latin. The world suddenly went crazy for his ideas. Even today it is thought that as much as 65 percent of Aristotle's original work may be lost forever.

How did Aristotle die?
According to an old legend, Aristotle drowned himself in the sea. The story goes that despair at not being able to explain the tides drove him to it. In reality, the ancient Greek died of natural causes.

"There is **nothing impossible**
to him who will try."

ALEXANDER THE GREAT

The son of a Macedonian king, my motto should have been "live fast, die young." To the Greeks, our people were hicks from the sticks — Macedon was a tiny kingdom, after all — but my old man soon had those Greeks under his thumb. He defeated their cities and we ruled their domain.

After he was assassinated, I set out to conquer the world . . . well, Persia — a vast empire stretching from Anatolia to the Indus Valley. I led my horsemen from the front, and my tiny army beat the Persians again and again. I conquered Egypt, then marched east into the heart of Persia. The Persian Empire collapsed and I was suddenly ruler of half of Asia. Some thought I must be a god, and who was I to argue?

Short-lived Glory
Then things went wrong. When I invaded India my weary army mutinied and forced me to turn back. When I married a beautiful Asian woman, Roxane, my generals said I was losing touch with my European roots. What would have happened, we'll never know, for I got sick and died, at only thirty-two. My generals fought over my legacy and my empire broke up as fast as it had been made.

TIMELINE

356 BCE Born the son of King Philip of Macedon

336 BCE Father assassinated

334 BCE Leads an invasion of the Persian Empire

331 BCE Destroys the Persian capital at Persepolis

326 BCE Invades northern India

323 BCE Dies of a fever in Babylon, modern-day Iraq

LEGACY

Alexander of Macedon was the greatest conqueror of the ancient world. By the age of twenty-five, he had defeated the mighty Persians in a series of epic battles, creating an empire of his own that stretched all the way from Greece to northern India.

WAR HORSE

Alexander's first love was his horse, Bucephalus. He won the fiery charger at the age of thirteen by proving himself the only person capable of riding it. The steed served him faithfully for eighteen years. Alexander was heartbroken when the horse died during his campaign in modern-day Pakistan.

SMART THINKING

In the city of Gordium, in modern-day Turkey, Alexander was shown a local wonder — a knotted rope that no one had ever been able to untie. Alexander solved the problem in an instant, by slicing the rope in two with his sword. Cutting the **Gordian Knot** is a good example of thinking outside the box.

?
Just how big was Alexander the Great's empire?
By the time of his death, Alexander is reckoned to have ruled an area covering over two million square miles (five million sq. km.). That is well over half the size of the United States today.

BATTLE VICTORIES

* At **Granicus,** in modern-day Turkey, Alexander won his first victory over the Persians, in 334 BCE.

* At **Issus,** in modern-day Turkey, he faced Persian emperor Darius III and beat him in 333 BCE.

* At **Gaugamela,** in modern-day Iraq, he defeated Darius again in 331 BCE — this time for good.

* At **Hydaspes,** in modern-day Pakistan, he beat Indian King Porus and his war elephants in 326 BCE.

"Give me a **firm place** to stand on and I will **move the Earth.**"

ARCHIMEDES

Yes, I'm the guy who jumped out of the bath and ran down the street, naked, shouting "Eureka!" ("I've found it!") It's what I'm best known for but, in fact, I should be remembered as one of the smartest people ever. I spent most of my life in Syracuse, a Greek port city in Sicily — we Greeks had cities all around the Mediterranean. My passion was math. Proving the relation between the surface area of a sphere and a cone was the sort of thing that really pushed my buttons! Would you believe I spent months calculating how many grains of sand it would take to fill the universe? It revealed all sorts of interesting stuff about big numbers and the distances of stars from the Earth.

Gadgets and Gizmos

I was a great inventor, too. I made a screw (named after me, of course) that let you pump water upward by turning a handle. And when the Romans besieged Syracuse by land and sea, I devised ingenious machines to fight them off. They eventually broke into the city, but I was too deep in geometry to notice. A Roman soldier didn't like it when I ignored him, and he stabbed me with his sword.

TIMELINE

ca. 287 BCE Born in Syracuse, on the present-day island of Sicily

ca. 213 BCE His machines defend Syracuse under siege by the Romans

ca. 212 BCE Killed by a Roman soldier at the end of the siege of Syracuse

MOVING THE WORLD

Archimedes studied levers. He worked out that, given a long enough lever, a human arm would be strong enough to shift the weight of the Earth. The only problem was managing to find a place outside the Earth on which the man with the lever could stand!

LEGACY

Archimedes was by far the greatest scientist, mathematician, and inventor of the ancient world. His devices included an early form of planetarium and a variety of unlikely weapons, including a giant claw for lifting enemy ships out of the water.

THAT "EUREKA" MOMENT

King Hiero of Syracuse asked Archimedes to find out whether or not a crown was made of pure gold. In order to get the answer, he needed to know the exact volume of the crown. Getting into his bathtub one day, he noticed the water level rose by the volume of his body. Now he could do the same with the crown: He realized that if he put it in the bathtub and saw how much water it displaced, he would be able to figure out its volume. Eureka!

BRAINY ANCIENTS

★ **Aristarchus** (ca. 310–230 BCE) was the first man to say that the Earth revolved around the sun, rather than vice versa.

★ **Eratosthenes** (ca. 276–195 BCE) tried to calculate the distance around the circumference of the Earth, and he almost got it right.

★ **Ptolemy** (ca. 90–168 CE) wrote important books about astronomy and geography.

?

Is it true that Archimedes used mirrors to set fire to enemy ships?
Ancient sources describe mirrors set up to concentrate the sun's rays so that enemy ships burst into flames. No one has managed to re-create the system in modern times, but it might well have existed.

"To have a great **peace**,
the state must be **united**."

QIN SHIHUANGDI

By the time of my birth, Chinese warlords had been fighting each other for 250 years. Historians called it the Warring States period, and that about summed it up. As a young man, I became King Zheng of Qin, and set about ending all wars. I defeated all the other states and paid officials to run the different regions. Then, as Qin Shihuangdi (First Emperor of China), I made sure I was the only person in the land who could have an army. Let's face it, there was only going to be one ruler, and that was going to be me. But having power went to my head and I began to worry about my enemies.

I burned almost all the books in China — to avoid being compared to past rulers — and any scholars caught with banned books were buried alive.

Wanting to Live Forever

I employed 700,000 men to build a vast mausoleum (a sort of city of death) around my grave. Then I thought I'd rather not die at all, so I traveled in search of secret potions to make me immortal. It was on one of these trips that I died. The Qin dynasty I founded lasted just four years after my death, but I would never be forgotten.

TIMELINE

ca. 259 BCE Born the son of the king of Qin, February 18

246 BCE Succeeds his father as ruler of Qin

221 BCE Proclaims himself First Emperor of China

220 BCE Orders building of the Great Wall

210 BCE Dies age forty-nine, September 10

LEGACY

Qin Shihuangdi was the first ruler to make China into a single state. If it weren't for his example, China might now be split into a number of different countries, just as Europe is. Since Qin, the idea of a unified China has never been forgotten.

THE GREAT WALL

Over the centuries, the Chinese had built sections of wall along their northern border to stop Mongolian horsemen from raiding Chinese towns and villages. Qin Shihuangdi decided to link these sections together to make one **Great Wall** that stretched for thousands of miles from the east of the country to the west.

? Where is Qin buried?

The body of Qin Shihuangdi is believed to lie in a vast underground tomb in Xi'an, Shaanxi province. Archaeologists have not yet tried to dig down into the tomb for fear of damaging treasures that lie within.

TERRACOTTA ARMY

Qin had more than seven thousand life-size sculptures of soldiers with horses and chariots buried in pits close to his tomb. Farmers discovered this **"Terracotta Army"** by chance in 1974 and it has become a major tourist attraction. The regiments of troops were meant to protect Qin in the afterlife.

QIN'S ACHIEVEMENTS

* Established one set of laws for the whole country.

* Standardized Chinese writing so people from different regions could understand one another.

* Built a network of roads and canals that enabled people and goods to move rapidly across the empire.

* Created a single currency for use throughout China.

"Veni, vidi, vici."
(I came, I saw, I conquered.)

JULIUS CAESAR

A Roman statesman of the highest order, I had always dreamed of being top dog (it was a dog-eat-dog world, after all). I was a great politician, for sure, but I really made my name as a general. I brought northern Europe under Roman rule, conquering the barbaric tribes of Gaul by fire and sword. I even invaded Britain — twice!

My victories brought me fame, but the Roman Senate got the idea that I was becoming too powerful. They weren't wrong! When they tried to fire me, I marched my army to Rome — I'd show them who was boss. I defeated their general, Pompey, and chased him to Egypt, where the pharaoh cut off his head just to please me. That didn't make me happy, so I overthrew him and put the beautiful Cleopatra on his throne instead.

An Error of Judgment

Back home, the people simply adored me. Carried away by my success, I proclaimed myself dictator-for-life. Big mistake! The senators accused me of wanting to be king and plotted my downfall. But did those cowards fight fair? No way! A bunch of them mobbed me and stabbed me to death in the Senate.

TIMELINE

ca. 100 BCE Born in Rome, modern-day Italy

59 BCE Elected consul, highest elected office in the Roman Republic

58–50 BCE Conquers Gaul

55–54 BCE Invades Britain (twice)

49–48 BCE Defeats Pompey

44 BCE Assassinated in Rome, March 15

FRIENDS

+ **Mark Antony** was Caesar's most loyal follower. After Caesar's assassination, Antony tracked down and killed the men responsible.

+ Egyptian pharaoh **Cleopatra** was romantically involved with Caesar.

+ Grand-nephew **Octavian** was Caesar's legal heir. He later became the first Roman emperor, Augustus.

LEGACY

Julius Caesar recognized that the ancient Roman political system was weak and corrupt. He set Rome on the road from being a republic, ruled by a Senate, to being an empire, with a single all-powerful ruler.

A VENGEFUL NATURE

While on a sea journey in 75 BCE, the young Caesar was captured and taken prisoner by pirates. As he was waiting for the ransom money for his release to arrive, Caesar joked and laughed with his captors. But after they let him go, he returned with a fleet, seized them, and crucified each and every one of them.

RIVALS

✗ **Vercingetorix** united the tribes of Gaul and led them in revolt against Caesar. He was defeated at Alesia in 52 BCE, and died a prisoner in Rome.

✗ **Pompey,** a one-time ally, thought that he should take over leadership of Rome.

✗ Once a friend, **Marcus Brutus** was among the senators who killed Caesar.

? What was the Julian calendar?

In 46 BCE, Caesar devised a calendar for which he invented "leap years." More accurate than any previous calendar, it was used across Europe for more than 1,500 years. The month of July was named in Caesar's honor.

"**No man** should be denied permission to follow the rites of the **Christians.**"

CONSTANTINE
THE GREAT

I was a Roman emperor and a Christian convert to boot. When I was young, my dad was one of three co-emperors appointed to help rule a tottering Roman Empire. Together, they tried to crush the fast-growing Christian religion using torture and executions. But my mom was a Christian, so I didn't know what to believe. When Dad died, I became his successor, controlling Britain and northern Europe. But there were three of us at the top — Maxentius ruling Italy and Licinius in the east — and I wanted the empire all to myself. I started with Maxentius and defeated him at the Milvian Bridge outside Rome in 312. Twelve years later I beat Licinius, too. You sure had to be a tough soldier to get to the top in the Roman Empire!

My Change of Faith

The night before I clashed with Maxentius in 312, I had this crazy vision of the Christian symbol of the cross. I made my soldiers paint crosses on their shields and we won the battle against the odds. That sure convinced me! As ruler of the Roman Empire I built churches, gave Christians tax breaks, and brought bishops to the center of power.

TIMELINE

ca. 272 CE Born at Naissus in modern-day Serbia, February 27

306 CE Self-proclaimed emperor of the western Roman Empire

312 CE Defeats his rival Maxentius at the Battle of the Milvian Bridge

313 CE Gives Christians favored status by the Edict of Milan

324 CE Acknowledged as sole ruler of the Roman Empire

337 CE Dies at Nicomedia in modern-day Turkey, May 22

LEGACY

Constantine the Great was the first Roman emperor to convert to Christianity. By favoring the Christian faith over other beliefs, he transformed the religion from a persecuted minority cult into the main belief of the Roman Empire.

ST. HELENA

Constantine's mother, Helena, was originally a servant girl. Like many poor people in the Roman Empire, she was Christian. Constantine made his mother an important figure in his empire. He sent her to supervise the restoration of the holy places in Palestine. There, she is said to have discovered the True Cross on which Jesus was crucified.

?
Why the sudden change in faith?

The story goes that, along with his vision of the cross, Constantine saw the words **"Hoc signo vinces"** — "with this sign, you will conquer." When his soldiers won the battle wearing the cross, he decided to become a Christian.

FOUNDING CONSTANTINOPLE

Constantine created a new capital for the Roman Empire at Byzantium in modern-day Turkey. Named after him, Constantinople flourished as a great Christian city and the capital of the Byzantine Empire for over one thousand years. Today, Constantinople is called Istanbul and is predominantly Muslim.

CHRISTIANITY: THE UPS AND DOWNS

* The Great Persecution is instigated by Roman Emperor Diocletian (ruled 284–305).

* Constantine (ruled 324–337) gave Christians most favored status.

* Emperor Julian (ruled 360–363) tried to restore the traditional "pagan" gods.

* Emperor Theodosius I (ruled 379–395) made Christianity the sole religion of the empire.

"He was a man born into the world
to shake all nations."

ATTILA THE HUN

My enemies called me "the scourge of God." One wrote that the grass never grew where my horse had trod. Good one! My people were the Huns, fearsome nomads from Asia. Always on the move, we ate, drank, and slept on horseback — seriously! We refused to honor the borders of states or empires. Instead we plagued innocent settlers in villages, towns, and cities. We'd turn up, we'd kill, loot, and burn, and then we'd move on. We so totally destroyed some places that no traces were left. We'd simply erased them from the map.

Bully Tactics

The Romans despised us as "barbarians," but their empire was crumbling. As leader of the Huns, I made Rome my enemy. I marauded and raided at will, striking terror wherever I went. In France, the empire fought back and had the gall to beat me at Chalons. I set my sights on Italy instead, burning cities to the ground. Rome itself lay at my mercy now. The Romans sent Pope Leo I to beg me to spare them. Well, by that time my men were sick and hungry, so I agreed to go home. After my death, my empire fell apart as my kids fought over its future.

TIMELINE

ca. 400 Born in Hungary

434 Becomes leader of the Huns

451 Defeated by Romans at Chalons

452 Invades Italy

453 Persuaded by Pope Leo I to spare Rome

454 Dies at his palace in modern-day Hungary

BARBARIC WAYS

According to the Romans, any people from outside the empire were known as "barbarians." In its decline, the empire was invaded by increasing numbers of these peoples, including Visigoths, Ostrogoths, Franks, and Vandals, as well as Huns. Although many barbarians settled inside the empire — and were even recruited to fight for the Romans — the Huns proved too wild to do likewise.

LEGACY

Through numerous merciless raids, Attila and his Huns severely weakened the Roman Empire. They dominated a large area from central Asia into western Europe, where they ruled through terror and destruction.

FAST FACTS

* Attila's warriors brought smallpox to Europe. The killer disease caused thousands more deaths than the Huns did.

* Some say that Attila died of a nosebleed.

* Attila was buried in a triple coffin of gold, silver, and lead. The slaves who buried him were executed so that they couldn't betray the location of his grave.

RIVALS

✖ **Fritigern,** a chieftain of the Goths, defeated and killed Roman emperor Valens at Adrianople in 378.

✖ **Alaric,** the king of the Visigoths, sacked Rome in 410.

✖ **Genseric,** king of the Vandals, looted Rome in 455.

✖ **Odoacer,** a Germanic warlord, deposed the last emperor in Rome in 476.

?

What made the Huns such good fighters?
Trained as hunters, the Huns fought on horseback, using powerful bows to fire arrows from the saddle. They ran circles around their enemies, who usually fought on foot with swords and lances.

2

THE MIDDLE AGES AND THE RENAISSANCE

800
CHARLEMAGNE CROWNED
The Holy Roman Empire is born when Charlemagne is crowned its first emperor.

1066
FRENCH INVASION
William the Conqueror is crowned King of England.

1206
MONGOL RULE
Genghis Khan founds the Mongol Empire, soon to become the largest empire the world has ever seen.

1325
AFRICAN GOLD
Mansa Musa puts Mali on the map as a center of great wealth and learning.

1431
SAINT JOAN
Joan of Arc is burned at the stake in France for defending king and country.

742–814
CHARLEMAGNE

ca. 1027–1087
WILLIAM THE CONQUEROR

ca. 1167–1227
GENGHIS KHAN

ca. 1280–1337
MANSA MUSA

1412–1431
JOAN OF ARC

The superstars of the Middle Ages busied themselves with building empires, and Genghis Khan ruled over the largest of them all. Then Joan of Arc became a martyr for trying to save her king and country. With the Renaissance came another kind of hero — the one led by curiosity. Columbus, da Vinci, Galileo, and Newton began to push new boundaries in the fields of discovery, the arts, and the sciences. Under their influence the world saw life in a different light.

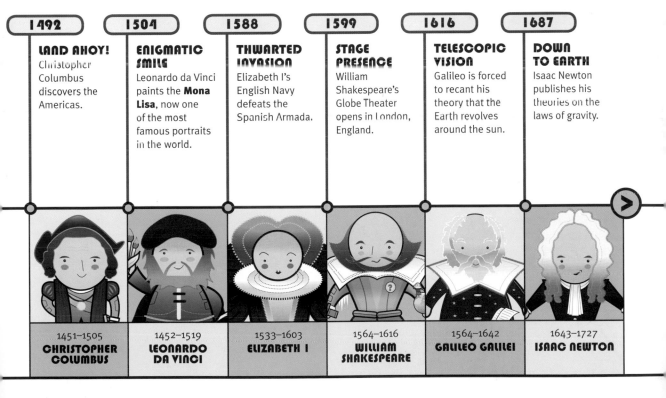

1492
LAND AHOY!
Christopher Columbus discovers the Americas.

1504
ENIGMATIC SMILE
Leonardo da Vinci paints the **Mona Lisa**, now one of the most famous portraits in the world.

1588
THWARTED INVASION
Elizabeth I's English Navy defeats the Spanish Armada.

1599
STAGE PRESENCE
William Shakespeare's Globe Theater opens in London, England.

1616
TELESCOPIC VISION
Galileo is forced to recant his theory that the Earth revolves around the sun.

1687
DOWN TO EARTH
Isaac Newton publishes his theories on the laws of gravity.

1451–1505
CHRISTOPHER COLUMBUS

1452–1519
LEONARDO DA VINCI

1533–1603
ELIZABETH I

1564–1616
WILLIAM SHAKESPEARE

1564–1642
GALILEO GALILEI

1643–1727
ISAAC NEWTON

"In order to **do** what is right,
we must **know** what is right."

CHARLEMAGNE

My name means "Charles the Great" and it's a moniker that suits me well. My people were the Franks. Half German, half French, they carved out a territory for themselves in the chaos that followed the fall of the mighty Roman Empire. My father, Pepin the Short, was their king.

I was both a fighting man and a Christian. I spread the word of God with fire and sword, crushing the heathen Saxons in wars lasting thirty years. Having conquered most of western Europe, my crowning moment came in Rome in 800 CE. On Christmas Day, Pope Leo III put a crown on my head,

knelt at my feet, and declared me Emperor of the Romans. The Holy Roman Empire was born!

Good Intentions

Though ruthless in battle, my ambitions went beyond fighting — I just wanted folks to learn. I ruled from Aachen, a real center of civilization, where I employed educated men to copy old manuscripts and advance learning across the land. After I died, my kids squabbled and, for a while, it looked like my empire was doomed, but it was still there one thousand years later.

TIMELINE

742 Born the son of Pepin the Short, April 2

768 Becomes co-ruler of the Frankish kingdom

771 Declares himself sole King of the Franks

800 Crowned Emperor of the Romans

814 Dies in his palace at Aachen, January 28

LEGACY

Charlemagne was the first emperor to rule western Europe in more than three hundred years. Although he spread Christianity throughout the region, he did so brutally. Those who refused to give up their old gods were massacred.

AN UNUSUAL GIFT

Caliph Haroun al-Rashid, Muslim ruler of the Middle East, wanted an alliance with Charlemagne. He sent him an elephant as a present. Coming from Baghdad, the animal reached Aachen in 801. No elephant had been seen in Europe for centuries, so the Caliph's gift was greeted by cheering crowds.

THIRST FOR BATTLE

* **772** Fights the Saxons (and again in 775–777, 782–785, and 792–803!)
* **773–774** Defeats the Lombards in northern Italy.
* **778** Invades Muslim-ruled Spain.
* **778** Attacks Bavaria.
* **796** Crushes the nomadic pagan Avars in the Danube region.

? Was Charlemagne French?

Although France is named after his people — the Franks — Charlemagne was as much German as French. The Franks were a Germanic tribe and Charlemagne's palace was at Aachen, in modern-day Germany.

FRIENDS

✚ **Roland** (d. 778) was one of Charlemagne's military commanders. His death in battle at Roncesvalles became the subject of a famous legend in later centuries.

✚ **Alcuin of York** (735–804) was an English scholar who served at Charlemagne's court. He was described as "the most learned man anywhere to be found."

"Life yields only to the **CONQUEROR.**
Never accept what can be gained by **giving in.**"

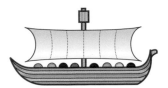

WILLIAM THE CONQUEROR

An angry young man, I grew up in medieval France. By the age of twenty, my armored fist was feared by all. I lost no battle, nor did I fail to capture castles — I crushed anyone who stood in my way.

Invading England

My title was Duke of Normandy, northern France, but I had a legitimate claim to the throne of England. The English favored Harold Godwinson as their ruler — an Anglo–Saxon and one of their own. In 1066, I gathered an army on the French coast and built a fleet to carry my knights and horses across the English Channel. It was Harold's bad luck that he faced another invasion in the north of his kingdom just as mine was starting. By the time he'd marched south, my boys were ashore. We clashed at Hastings and Harold was killed — perhaps by an arrow in the eye. His army fled and the rest, as they say, is history.

I had myself crowned king in Westminster Cathedral on Christmas Day and set out to rule England with a rod of iron. I parceled out the land to my followers, built castles to dominate the country, and mercilessly stamped out rebellion. I had conquered the English in every sense.

TIMELINE

ca. 1027 Born the illegitimate son of the Duke of Normandy

1035 Becomes Duke of Normandy at eight years of age

1066 Defeats Harold at Hastings and is crowned King of England

1087 Dies after a fall from his horse at Nantes, France

DOMESDAY BOOK

In 1085, King William I ordered a detailed survey of his kingdom. He wanted to know the number of people and livestock, how land was used, and what it was worth. The results were written down in the **Domesday Book**. It tells us that England had a population of two million people — fifty million fewer people than it does today.

LEGACY

William, Duke of Normandy, became the first Norman king of England in 1066. His followers and their successors ruled England for many centuries. They introduced changes to the English language and culture that remain in evidence up to the present day.

GORY DETAILS

* Several bishops fought for William at Hastings. Because churchmen were banned from shedding blood, they carried clubs — to beat enemies to death without cutting them.

* During William's burial, in Caen, Normandy, his corpse's stomach exploded, covering everyone in horrible goo and releasing a foul stink.

BAYEUX TAPESTRY

An embroidery was made to celebrate William's conquest. Called the **Bayeux Tapestry**, it measures 230 feet (70 meters) long. Presented like a comic strip, it shows scene after scene of Norman horsemen with spears fighting Anglo–Saxon axemen. It is kept in the town of Bayeux in Normandy, but was probably made in England.

?

Was the conquest good for England?

At first, the Norman Conquest was a disaster for the Anglo Saxon English. The Normans stole their land and treated them like slaves. But William brought progress too, with new stone buildings, better ways of farming, and strong government.

"I have united the **whole world** in **one** empire."

GENGHIS KHAN

Known in my youth as Temujin, I was a fatherless horseman living among the nomads of the Asian steppe. When we weren't hunting, we were fighting each other. You had to watch your back to stay alive. I was both ruthless and smart, seeking friends and allies, while crushing enemies without mercy.

Lord of All
I wanted to end the tribal infighting and turn our aggression outward. If everyone followed my vision, what a force we'd be! At a great meeting in 1206, tribal leaders acknowledged me as Genghis Khan, which means "Lord of All." United, my swarms of horsemen struck to the east and the west, sacking the capital of the Chinese Empire and the rich Silk Road cities of Bokhara and Samarkand. We paralyzed our enemies with the speed of our attacks and terrorized them with our battle cries.

We massacred thousands, but don't go thinking I was a savage. I respected the religions of the countries I conquered and imposed humane laws. Where I ruled, there was order and safety. I had the skill to found an empire that would go on expanding long after my death. I'm a legend to this day.

TIMELINE

ca. 1167 Born with the name Temujin in Mongolia

1190 Leads the Mongol confederation

1206 Recognized as sole leader of all the steppe tribes

1211 Invades China

1227 Dies in August at Yinchuan, northwest China

LEGACY
A skilled leader, Genghis Khan founded the great Mongol Empire. Through murderous conquests, he created the largest land empire the world has ever seen. Reaching from China to eastern Europe, it covered one-fifth of Earth's total landmass.

THE SILK ROAD
The Mongol Empire allowed traders to travel safely overland between Europe and China. This route was called the **Silk Road**, because Chinese silk was one of the most valuable goods carried along it. Venetian Marco Polo (1254–1324) later traveled along the Silk Road and stayed at Kublai Khan's court in Beijing.

MONGOL MARVELS
✳ Mongols drank fermented mare's milk and fresh blood from cuts made in their horses' sides.

✳ Mongolian horses were small — a rider's feet almost touched the ground — but they could travel up to 100 miles (160 kilometers) a day, twice as far as most horses.

✳ Mongol commanders used smoke signals to send orders to their horsemen in battle.

?
Is it true that Mongol armor was made of silk?
Possibly! Stories tell of Mongols wearing silk tunics as protection against arrows. Many people thought this was a myth, but recent research shows that layers of silk can even stop bullets.

IN HIS FOOTSTEPS
★ **Kublai Khan** (1215–1294), Genghis's grandson, conquered the whole of China and ruled the region as emperor.

★ **Tamurlaine** (1336–1405) was inspired by the Mongol conquests to win an empire stretching from India to Turkey.

★ **The warrior Babur** (1483–1530), claiming descent from Genghis, founded the great Mogul Empire in India.

"The **most feared** by his enemies
and the **most able** to do good
for those around him."

MANSA MUSA

I ruled the great Mali Empire in West Africa, and yet the outside world hardly knew I existed. Well, think about it: My empire was separated from the cities of North Africa and Europe by the vast, empty spaces of the blistering Sahara desert.

Then, one fine day, I sprang one of history's great surprises. I suddenly appeared in Egypt, with five hundred servants and eighty camels carrying more gold than anyone had ever seen. What a sensation! A devout Muslim, I had decided to make a pilgrimage to Mecca, passing through Egypt on the way. Traveling in style just came naturally. By law, I was the owner of every nugget of gold found in my empire, and fortunately there was plenty to be found.

Cultural Lead
I wanted to turn Mali into one of the great centers of the Islamic world. I founded universities and libraries, bringing back scholars and their books from my travels. I attracted architects and builders to my empire, where they erected fine mosques in the cities of Gao and Timbuktu. In time, even distant Europe knew of me. Mali was on the map!

TIMELINE

ca. 1280 Born

1312 Becomes ruler of the Mali Empire

1324 Makes the city of Timbuktu part of his empire

1324–1325 Makes a pilgrimage to Mecca in Arabia

ca. 1337 Dies

TIMBUKTU
At the time of the great Mali Empire, **Timbuktu** was the city from which camel caravans set out on their journeys across the Sahara to Egypt or Morocco. Mansa Musa built a great mosque there, made of mud bricks and sand. Today it counts as one of the wonders of world architecture. Timbuktu's library contains hundreds of thousands of ancient manuscripts.

LEGACY
In the Middle Ages, Africa was a continent of wealth and learning. Mansa Musa's Mali Empire in West Africa was among the richest countries in the world. Musa went on to make it an important center of knowledge and teaching.

MUSA'S GOLD
* In Mansa Musa's time, Mali was the source of more than half the world's gold.
* On his journey to Mecca in 1324, Musa spent or gave away so much gold that it cut the value of the gold coins used for trade, causing a widespread financial crisis.

AFRICAN RIVALS
* The kingdom of **Benin**, famous for its beautiful bronze carvings, was in the rain forest south of Mali.
* Great **Zimbabwe**, centered on a large walled city, flourished in southern Africa at the time of the Mali Empire.
* Christian emperors ruled **Ethiopia** in east Africa.

?
What happened to Musa's empire?
Little more than one hundred years after Mansa Musa's death, Mali was in terminal decline. In the nineteenth century, the whole area came under French rule. Now independent, Mali is one of the world's poorest nations.

"I am **sent from God**, the King of Heaven,
to chase you **out of France**."

JOAN of ARC

A tough woman in a man's world, I was born a simple peasant in a French village. As a child working in the fields, I heard voices telling me to save my beloved country. The English were invading and the French people were angry, but our king, Charles VII, was not a very good leader.

Fresh Hope and Fighting Spirit

Inspired by my voices, I went to the king's court and persuaded him that I had been sent by God to save France. No one had ever seen a woman like me — I wore men's clothes and cut my hair short when all women wore it long. I gave orders to French generals and they obeyed me. I wrote letters to the English, telling them to leave France, and I called on the French people to rise up against the invaders.

We freed the city of Orléans from a siege and had King Charles VII crowned at Reims. My army won battle after battle. I was always in the thick of the action, and that was my downfall. English allies, the Burgundians, captured me and I was tried as a witch. I spoke out in court, but the trial was rigged. The English burned me at the stake in a market square in Rouen, when I was just nineteen years old.

TIMELINE

ca. 1412 Born at Domrémy, France, January 6

1424 Starts to hear voices

1429 Defeats the English at the siege of Orléans

1430 Is taken prisoner

1431 Burned at the stake as a heretic, May 30

LEGACY

At a time when women were expected to stay home, Joan of Arc led the armies of France to a series of stunning victories during the Hundred Years' War. Through her actions, Joan became a national hero, but her enemies (the English) burned her at the stake.

RIVALS

✖ **Henry VI** (1421–1471), the English king whose followers claimed his right to the French throne in 1422.

✖ **Philip the Good**, Duke of Burgundy (1396–1467), contested Charles VII's right to the French throne and made an alliance with the English. He sold Joan to them following her capture.

AFTERMATH

✳ Following Joan's execution, her captors burned her body twice more, to reduce it to ashes, and tipped her ashes into a river.

✳ Twenty years after Joan's death, a retrial ordered by the pope found her innocent.

✳ Joan was declared a saint by the Catholic Church in 1920.

? Why was Joan executed?

The main reason the court found for declaring Joan guilty was that she dressed as a man — "an abomination" according to a verse in the Bible. Really, she was executed because her enemies, chiefly the English, feared her power.

LONG WAR

Joan's battles were part of the **Hundred Years' War**, which actually lasted 116 years. The war started in 1337, when the English claimed the right to rule France. Joan's actions stopped the English just as it started to look as if they might win France. The tide turned and, by 1453, the French had claimed victory.

"Once **EVERYONE** made fun of my plan,
but now even tailors think they can
DISCOVER new lands."

CHRISTOPHER COLUMBUS

I was a believer! I believed you could sail west from Europe and reach the east of Asia. Anyone with a brain could see the Earth was round, but no European had thought of reaching India, China, or Japan by sailing into the sunset . . . before me, that is! I did my own calculations and decided it would work. But I had no cash and couldn't afford to go.

Royal Sponsors

I went to Spain's ruling duo, Ferdinand and Isabella, and promised them the world (or at least the bits I found) when they coughed up the money. With three ships and ninety men, I headed west in 1492. We spent five weeks on the ocean before we struck land. I wasn't sure where we were, but reckoned it must be a part of Japan. I sailed home to boast of finding a land of gold, and Ferdinand and Isabella sent me back to run the place. After that, it all went wrong. First I was arrested for abuse of power, then Ferdinand and Isabella cheated me over money. But I'd won my place in history, having made four voyages in all. Funny thing was, I died without realizing that what I'd found wasn't Asia at all, but a whole New World.

TIMELINE

1451 Born in Genoa, Italy

1492 First voyage, landing in the Bahamas, October 12

1493–1495 Second voyage; West Indies

1498 Third voyage; South America

1502–1504 Fourth voyage; Central America

1505 Dies in Valladolid, Spain

FAST FACTS

✳ Columbus usually used the Spanish version of his name: **Cristóbal Colón**.

✳ Columbus's three ships were called the **Niña**, the **Pinta**, and the **Santa María**.

✳ No one knows for sure where in the Bahamas Columbus first landed. It may have been on San Salvador, but Samana Cay or Grand Turk are other possibilities.

LEGACY

Columbus was not the first European to sail to the Americas — that was probably a Viking 500 years earlier — but his first voyage, in 1492, had a big impact on history. It paved the way for Europeans to colonize the New World.

CRIMES AGAINST HUMANITY

Columbus is an important explorer. His travels started the relationship between Europe and the Americas. But Columbus and his followers enslaved or massacred thousands of people they found living in the New World and forced large numbers of them to convert to Christianity.

FELLOW GLOBETROTTERS

★ **John Cabot** sailed from England to Newfoundland in 1497.

★ **Vasco da Gama** sailed from Portugal around Africa to India in 1498.

★ **Vasco Núñez de Balboa** crossed Panama to reach the Pacific coast in 1513.

★ **Ferdinand Magellan's** expedition sailed right around the globe from 1519 to 1522.

?

Why wasn't the New World named after Columbus?
Columbus himself refused to accept that he had discovered new territory. Meanwhile, Italian Amerigo Vespucci wrote an account of travels in the New World in the early 1500s. A mapmaker literally put Amerigo's name on the map by labeling the new continent America.

"**Wisdom** is the daughter of **experience**."

LEONARDO DA VINCI

Born a peasant in what is now Italy, I learned by looking closely at people and nature, not from reading books. I had the good fortune to be born near Florence, a city teeming with artists and thinkers. This was the Renaissance — minds were opening up to new ideas and anything seemed possible. Although I trained as a painter, art was never enough: I wanted to be an engineer, an inventor, a scientist.

Driven by Curiosity

In Rome I got hold of corpses and cut them up to study the inner workings of the body, although at the time this was both a sin and a crime. I was fascinated by movement, and sketched whirlwinds and flowing water. I filled countless notebooks with inventions that were way ahead of their time.

Some of the most powerful men in the world paid me, not just to decorate their palaces but to strengthen their castles and make machines for their wars. I admit, by the time I died, I hadn't actually painted that many pictures, neither had I invented many machines that could be built . . . but I will always be remembered as a wise man who probed deep into the mysteries of life.

TIMELINE

1452 Born near Florence, Italy, April 15

1477 Sets up his own artist's studio in Florence

1482 Works for Ludovico Sforza, son of ruling Duke of Milan

1504 Paints the **Mona Lisa**

1516 Employed by King François I of France

1519 Dies at Amboise, France, May 2

LEGACY

The quintessential "Renaissance man," Leonardo was astounding in many ways. As an artist he painted masterpieces, but he was also one of the founders of modern science as well as an inventor of imaginary machines.

LEONARDO'S MACHINES

In his notebooks, Leonardo da Vinci sketched:

* A winged machine that would allow a man to fly like a bird.
* A helicopter, based on observation of spinning airborne seeds.
* An armored man-powered vehicle, like a tank.
* A diving suit with helmet and breathing tube.
* A portable bridge.

FAMOUS WORKS

* The smiling **Mona Lisa** is Leonardo's most famous painting.
* **The Last Supper** is a wall painting in Milan.
* The mysterious **Virgin of the Rocks** exists as two almost identical paintings.
* The magical **Vitruvian Man** is a nude figure drawn inside a square and a circle.

? What was the Renaissance?

It means "rebirth," and describes the time between 1400 and 1600, when artists and thinkers in Europe created a cultural revolution. It produced a flood of new ideas as well as many innovative paintings and sculptures.

RIVALS

* **Michelangelo** (1475–1564) was a sculptor, painter, poet, and architect. His most famous work is the painted ceiling of the Sistine Chapel in the Vatican.
* **Raphael** (1483–1520) was a great painter who worked chiefly in Rome. He also decorated rooms in the Vatican.

"I have the **body** of a weak and feeble woman,
but I have the **heart** and stomach of a king."

ELIZABETH I

I had to learn early on in life that only the tough survive: First Dad had Mom's head chopped off, then my sister, Queen Mary, locked me up in the Tower of London. We weren't a loving family. When I became queen, the big question was whether England should be a Catholic or Protestant country. I was Protestant. My enemies wanted to replace me with my Catholic cousin, Mary, Queen of Scots, so I kept her locked up for eighteen years and then cut off her head. It was a family tradition, after all.

A Reign to Remember

In 1588, the Catholic king of Spain sent his Armada to invade England, but it failed and my popularity soared. I encouraged adventurers like Francis Drake and Walter Raleigh to sail across the oceans. My sailors could act like pirates, as long as they gave me a cut of their profits.

They called me the Virgin Queen, because I never married, and the name of England's first colony in America (Virginia) celebrates that very fact. In the end, I left England a far greater country than I had found it and countless paintings and poems honored my reign.

TIMELINE

1533 Born daughter of King Henry VIII in London, England, September 7

1536 Her mother, Anne Boleyn, is executed

1558 Comes to the throne on the death of her sister, Mary

1587 Has her cousin Mary, Queen of Scots, executed

1588 The Spanish Armada is defeated

1603 Dies, March 24

SPANISH ARMADA

In 1588, Spanish King Philip II sent a vast fleet of warships to invade England in an attempt to throw Elizabeth off the throne. The English navy attacked this **Armada** with cannon and fire ships. The Spanish were forced to abandon the invasion. Many of their ships were destroyed by storms on the way home.

LEGACY

Queen Elizabeth I ruled England for 45 years. She was strong and ruthless in meeting a host of dangers at home and abroad. English talent flourished during her reign — from William Shakespeare's plays to the voyages of Sir Francis Drake.

MEET THE FAMILY

★ **Henry VII** (reigned 1485–1509) was Elizabeth's grandfather and founder of the Tudor dynasty.

★ **Henry VIII** (reigned 1509–47) was Elizabeth's father. He had six wives and executed two of them.

★ **Anne Boleyn** (1501–1536), Elizabeth's mother, was executed for failing to produce a son.

★ **Edward VI** (reigned 1547–53), Elizabeth's half-brother, died aged fifteen.

★ **Mary I** (reigned 1553–58), Elizabeth's Catholic sister.

GREAT ELIZABETHANS

★ **Sir Francis Drake** (1540–1596) was a swashbuckling sailor who fought the Spanish. He sailed around the world and was knighted on his return in 1580.

★ **Sir Walter Raleigh** (1554–1618) was authorized by Elizabeth to found the colony of Virginia in 1584. Accused of plotting against her successor, King James I, he was executed.

?

Why didn't Elizabeth marry?
Men lined up to propose, yet Elizabeth always turned them down. While marriage could have produced an heir or sealed a powerful alliance, a husband would have wanted to share power, and Elizabeth was determined to rule alone.

"Some are **born** great, some **achieve** greatness, and some have greatness **thrust** upon them."

WILLIAM SHAKESPEARE

Was I or was I not? That is the question. I'm one of the world's most famous writers, yet some people claim I never penned a thing. Well, I can't prove that I did, so you'll just have to take my word for it.

An Actor's Life

Drifting from my hometown of Stratford to the city of London, I plunged into the theatrical world, acting here and writing plays there. The Lord Chamberlain's Men, that's me and my actors, built our own theater, the Globe, where we entertained both the cultured elite and a ragged mob of commoners. Money poured in (some ending up in my pocket) and words poured out of me in torrents — dramatic speeches, romantic speeches, puns and philosophy, slapstick and tragedy. I created some of the most memorable characters who never lived: funny Falstaff, hesitant Hamlet, murderous Macbeth, and romantic Romeo. I wrote 38 plays in all (OK, I had help with some of them) and 154 sonnets. Pretty good, I'd say. No wonder some claim one single man couldn't have done it all, especially a simple merchant's son from Stratford. Well, I did, I tell you. Believe me now?

TIMELINE

1564 Born in Stratford-upon-Avon, England, April 23

1582 Marries Anne Hathaway

1593 First published poem, **Venus and Adonis**

1594 Joins Lord Chamberlain's Men theater company

1599 Globe Theater opens in London

1616 Dies, April 23

LEGACY

Shakespeare is one of the greatest poets and playwrights who ever lived. He was the superstar of an era when English theater was flourishing as never before (or since). His plays are still performed worldwide and a number have been made into movies.

WHAT'S HIS NAME?

Shakespeare may have been a great writer, but he often had trouble spelling his own name. He wrote it as Shaksper, Shakespere, Shakespear, Shakspeare, Shackspeare, Shakspere, Shaxspere, and a dozen other variants.

THE GLOBE THEATER

Many of Shakespeare's plays were performed at the **Globe Theater**, in London. Made of wood and straw, the building burned down in 1613, after a cannon fired onstage during a performance of Shakespeare's **Henry VIII** set it alight. A reconstructed Globe Theater opened in 1997, near the site of the original.

QUOTABLE QUOTES

Among the most quoted Shakespeare lines are:

✽ "To be or not to be, that is the question . . ." (**Hamlet**).

✽ "All the world's a stage . . ." (**As You Like It**).

✽ "Now is the winter of our discontent . . ." (**Richard III**).

✽ "Is this a dagger which I see before me?" (**Macbeth**).

? Did Shakespeare write Shakespeare?

Some people claim that William Shakespeare didn't have the education to write so many superb works. They suggest someone more cultured and higher placed in society must have written them. But there is still no solid evidence for anyone writing Shakespeare's plays . . . except Shakespeare!

"The **authority** of a thousand is not worth
the **reasoning** of a single individual."

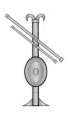

GALILEO GALILEI

While some looked for truth in the Bible and others in the works of Aristotle, I was the sort who needed to see and think for himself. God gave us senses and a brain — surely he intended us to use them! Of course, people had written about the moon, the sun, and the stars before, but I made a telescope so that I could observe them closely. I was interested in movement, you see. I timed objects falling and pendulums swinging, and impressed people when I calculated the exact path of a cannonball, so that gunners could be more accurate.

Battling with the Catholic Church

While I was looking at God's universe and thinking about what I saw, the Church took a different view. They rejected my idea that the Earth moved around the sun. I was certain that it did but, in 1616, I publicly denied it for fear of torture by the dreaded Inquisition. Even so, I still couldn't stop writing about it and finally the inquisitors found me guilty of heresy. They put me under arrest for the rest of my life. They refused to look through my telescope, of course. Had they seen what I could see, things might have turned out differently.

TIMELINE

1564 Born in Pisa, Italy, February 15

1581 Carries out first experiments, with pendulums

1609 Makes his first telescope

1616 Forced to recant his theory that the Earth moves around the sun

1633 Inquisition finds him guilty of heresy

1642 Dies near Florence, Italy, January 8

THE APPLIANCE OF SCIENCE

Through his observations, Galileo made a number of significant discoveries:

✳ That objects dropped in a vacuum will fall at the same rate, regardless of their weight.

✳ That a pendulum can be used to make a clock.

✳ That he could make a telescope that would magnify twenty times.

✳ That the planet Jupiter has moons revolving around it.

LEGACY

Galileo has been dubbed "the father of science." He used experiments and math to explore the movement of objects ranging from cannonballs to planets. His argument that the Earth moved around the sun got him locked up by the Catholic Inquisition.

DOWN TO EARTH

It is often said that Galileo dropped objects from great heights to record their movements as they fell to Earth. On one such occasion, he is said to have dropped a feather and a cannonball from the Leaning Tower of Pisa in an attempt to prove they would hit the ground at the same time. It's a great story, but sadly it's almost certainly not true!

RIVALS

✘ **Nicolaus Copernicus** (1473–1543) was a Polish astronomer who placed the sun — and not the Earth — at the center of the universe.

✘ **Johannes Kepler** (1571–1630) was a German astronomer who accurately described the movement of planets around the sun and realized that the moon caused ocean tides.

?

What was the Inquisition?
The Inquisition was a body set up by the Catholic Church to stamp out allegedly false beliefs (heresy). Astronomer Giordano Bruno was burned at the stake in 1600 for saying that the sun was a star. It seems Galileo got off lightly!

"To every action there is an equal and opposite reaction."

ISAAC NEWTON

Call me a super-geek, a nerd if you like, I don't care. I never had much time for people. I rarely spoke, had no friends, and often forgot to eat. Science was my thing. I invented an improved telescope and my optical experiments showed how ordinary light contained all the colors of the rainbow. I even went as far as poking a bodkin (a type of needle) behind my eye — just to see how it altered my vision!

The Pull of Gravity

Most people just accepted that, if you dropped something, it fell to the ground. But why shouldn't it fall upward? I was convinced that math could help explain the natural world. Then, one fine day, an apple fell from a tree and everything dropped into place — quite literally. I realized that a single force held the planets in orbit around the sun and made things fall toward the Earth. I called this force "gravity," and although it didn't really make sense — it was invisible, after all — I knew it had to exist, because all my calculations said so. My laws of motion made the world seem rational and predictable. My ideas began the Age of Reason and I was worshiped for it.

TIMELINE

1642 Born in Lincolnshire, England, December 25

1667 Becomes a fellow of Trinity College, Cambridge, England

1687 Publishes the **Principia Mathematica**

1703 Elected president of the Royal Society

1704 Publishes his **Opticks**, a book about light

1727 Dies in London, March 20

LEGACY

Isaac Newton is famous for discovering the force of gravity. It explained both the movement of the planets and why objects on Earth fell downward. Newton made people believe that the whole universe was a mechanism governed by natural laws.

QUIRKY FELLOW

* Newton tried to calculate the day on which the world would end. Using the prophecies of Daniel in the Bible, he reckoned 2060 was the likeliest year.

* In his later years, Newton became Master of the Mint, in charge of England's currency. He used to tour London pubs looking for counterfeit coins.

NEWTON'S ACHIEVEMENTS

* Discovered gravity, explaining the motion of the planets and of falling bodies on Earth.

* Stated the three laws of motion in his book, **Principia Mathematica**.

* Showed that white light contains the colors of the rainbow.

* Founded the branch of math called calculus.

?

Is it true that Newton's apple fell on his head?
The famous story of the apple is mostly true. Newton often said the idea of gravity came to him when he was sitting in a garden and saw an apple fall. It didn't actually fall on his head, though.

RIVALS

✖ **René Descartes** (1596–1650), a French philosopher who invented his own theory of motion that rivaled Newton's. It was wrong.

✖ **Gottfried Leibniz** (1646–1716) argued with Newton over which of them invented calculus.

✖ **John Flamsteed** (1646–1719), Astronomer Royal. The pair fell out after disagreeing about the nature of a comet that appeared in 1680.

3 REVOLUTION AND THE ENLIGHTENMENT

1661
THE SUN KING
Louis XIV rules France as an absolute king, promoting industry, science, and the arts.

1789
INDEPENDENT AMERICA
George Washington becomes the first president of the United States.

1796
RUSSIA ENLIGHTENED
Empress Catherine dies, having led Russia through a golden age.

1804
A NEW ORDER
Napoleon Bonaparte crowns himself Emperor of France and gains control over most of Europe.

1813
LATIN LIBERATOR
Simón Bolívar sets South America on the road to liberation from Spanish rule.

1638–1715
LOUIS XIV

1732–1799
GEORGE WASHINGTON

1729–1796
CATHERINE THE GREAT

1769–1821
NAPOLEON BONAPARTE

1783–1830
SIMÓN BOLÍVAR

The superstars of this era were visionaries whose actions did much to improve the lives of others, if not immediately, then in the years to come. This was a time of great learning and of social and political reform across the globe — from Russia, through Europe, to South America. Meanwhile, the United States gained independence from Britain, only to risk losing everything in a bloody civil war, from which it emerged stronger than ever.

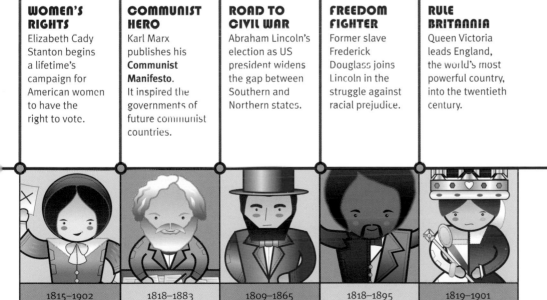

1848
WOMEN'S RIGHTS
Elizabeth Cady Stanton begins a lifetime's campaign for American women to have the right to vote.

1848
COMMUNIST HERO
Karl Marx publishes his **Communist Manifesto**. It inspired the governments of future communist countries.

1860
ROAD TO CIVIL WAR
Abraham Lincoln's election as US president widens the gap between Southern and Northern states.

1861
FREEDOM FIGHTER
Former slave Frederick Douglass joins Lincoln in the struggle against racial prejudice.

1900
RULE BRITANNIA
Queen Victoria leads England, the world's most powerful country, into the twentieth century.

1815–1902
ELIZABETH CADY STANTON

1818–1883
KARL MARX

1809–1865
ABRAHAM LINCOLN

1818–1895
FREDERICK DOUGLASS

1819–1901
QUEEN VICTORIA

"I am the state."

LOUIS XIV

Known as the Sun King, I was the all-powerful ruler of France. I built and lived in the greatest palace in Europe — the ultralong Hall of Mirrors with its 375 mirrors still wows visitors today.

Life wasn't always this glittering. When I was a child-king, the French rebelled in an uprising called the Fronde. I was forced to flee from Paris and live on the run. After the rebellion ended, I vowed it would never happen again. Once I grew up, I made sure no one could challenge my rule. I claimed to hold the throne as God's appointee, and exercised absolute power. What I said went and, for a time, my people liked it. I promoted industry and encouraged the sciences and arts. I used the work of painters and architects to spread my image of power and glory.

Tarnishing My Reputation

Then I went a step too far. As a Catholic, I cracked down on Protestants. I destroyed their churches and schools and drove hundreds of thousands into exile. Waging endless, costly wars around France's borders, I bankrupted the state and reduced my people to starvation. Being the most magnificent monarch in Europe had certainly come at a price.

TIMELINE

1638 Born, September 5

1643 Becomes king of France, aged four

1661 Takes over personal rule

1682 Royal court moves to Versailles

1685 Revokes the Edict of Nantes

1715 Dies, September 1

LEGACY

Louis XIV was France's most famous king, reigning for longer than any monarch of any major European country (seventy-two years, one hundred and ten days). He ruled as an absolute king, without a strong parliament or legal limits to his power.

PALACE DAYS

Life at Louis's palace of **Versailles** revolved around the Sun King. When he woke in the morning, nobles crowded into his bedchamber. They followed him around all day, until he went to bed surrounded by the same crowd. The nobles spent their time gossiping and backbiting among themselves but did not plot revolt.

HAIR TODAY, GONE TOMORROW

* Louis XIV was known for wearing wigs. He wore them to hide the fact that he was going bald at a young age.

* Employing some forty-eight wigmakers, Louis had more than one thousand wigs in all.

* The wig soon became a must-have accessory for members of the French nobility.

?

What was the Edict of Nantes?
It was an agreement, made in 1598, that ended religious wars in France by granting tolerance to Huguenots (French Protestants). In 1685, Louis XIV revoked the edict, making Protestant worship illegal. It is seen as one of his biggest mistakes.

LOUIS'S ALL-STARS

* ★ **Jean Racine** (1639–1699), an influential poet and author of French stage tragedies.

* ★ **Molière** (1622–1673), a writer of many plays, often quoted as the father of modern French comedy.

* ★ **Vauban** (1633–1707), an ingenious military engineer. He built thirty-seven impenetrable French fortresses.

* ★ **Jules Hardouin-Mansart** (1646–1708), an architect. He designed the palace at Versailles.

"Honesty is always the **best policy**."

GEORGE WASHINGTON

Solid and honest, I was not the type either to rule or to rebel. I preferred a quiet life on my Virginia estate, Mount Vernon. But the way the British treated their American colonies offended my sense of right and wrong. When called upon, I agreed to lead an army to fight for independence in the American Revolution. The odds were against us but, with help from the French, we won.

The First US President

Some people thought the United States needed a military strongman to take power and impose order on the new country. I was the person they had in mind, but I had not rebelled against a king in order to become a king myself. All I wanted now was to retire to Mount Vernon and live in peace.

Still, I did my duty and oversaw the drawing up of a fair and workable Constitution. Twice I was elected president — the first time without a single vote against me in the Electoral College. I kept the country out of a war that broke out in Europe — America was to be a peaceful nation. Two terms in office were enough for me, though. I finally got that retirement I'd dreamed of.

TIMELINE

1732 Born in Virginia, February 22

1754–1758 Fights in the French and Indian War

1775–1783 Commander-in-chief in the American Revolution

1789 Becomes first US president

1797 Retires after a second term

1799 Dies at Mount Vernon, Virginia, December 14

WASHINGTON SMARTS

✳ A very big man, the first US president took a size 13 shoe.

✳ Washington's favorite sport was foxhunting.

✳ He wore dentures, not made of wood, as some say, but of ivory, real teeth, and gold.

✳ Washington gave the shortest-ever inaugural address. It lasted a mere ninety seconds.

LEGACY

Known as "the father of his country," Washington was the first president of the United States. He commanded the colonists during the American Revolution and went on to lead the country on the path to stability and democracy.

THAT LEGENDARY TREE

Every child knows that, as a boy, Washington chopped down a cherry tree and then confessed to it because he could not tell a lie. Sadly, there is no truth to this story. It was made up by Parson Mason Weems in a book he wrote on Washington a year after the president's death.

FRIENDS

✚ **Thomas Jefferson** (1743–1826), the main author of the Declaration of Independence, served as Washington's first Secretary of State. He was later elected the third US president.

✚ **Benjamin Franklin** (1706–1790), American scientist, patriot, and diplomat, was a close friend and supporter of Washington during the American Revolution.

?

Did Washington own slaves?
Like most Virginia landowners in his time, Washington owned slaves. He inherited his first slaves at eleven years of age. Later in life, he realized that slavery was wrong and favored its gradual abolition. He freed all his slaves upon his death.

"It is better to be **subject** to one master than **subservient** to many."

CATHERINE THE GREAT

I'd like to meet any man who still thinks women are the weaker sex — I'd eat him for breakfast! I was born a German princess, which sounds great, but my family only ruled a tiny, poor statelet. Aged sixteen, I married Peter III, heir to the throne of mighty Russia. No one asked me what I thought.

Girl Power

I loathed my husband. He was a feeble bully, a man who played with toy soldiers. I was not the only person who hated him, either. Soon after he became emperor, he was assassinated. Yes, I was pleased, but don't go thinking I was behind his murder! The plotters who killed Peter III put me on the throne in his place. They didn't really expect me to run the country, but I wouldn't be bossed around: I refused to let my son, Paul, take over when he grew up and I was careful never to marry again.

Most Russians were serfs — peasants owned by the nobility. They were not happy with their lot, but when they rioted against me, I crushed them. Meanwhile, I ordered war after war to expand Russia's borders. I may not have given my people freedom, but I left the country stronger than I had found it.

TIMELINE

1729 Born in Stettin, Prussia, May 2; named Sophie Friederike Auguste von Anhalt-Zerbst-Dornburg

1745 Marries the heir to the Russian throne, Peter III

1762 Crowned Empress Catherine II after her husband Peter III is assassinated

1796 Dies, November 17

LEGACY

Catherine the Great wielded absolute rule over her country, and used her power to carry out reforms. In her bid to modernize Russia, so that it was more in line with Western European countries, she led Russia through a Golden Age.

FRIENDS

+ **Count Grigory Orlov** (1734–1783) was romantically linked to Catherine at the time her husband was murdered. Grigory's brother Alexei was the assassin.

+ **Prince Grigory Potemkin** (1739–1791) was commander-in-chief of Catherine's army.

+ French philosopher **Voltaire** (1694–1778) admired Catherine as an "enlightened despot," for using her absolute power to pass beneficial reforms.

ENEMIES

✘ **Yemelyan Pugachev** (1742–1775) was a Cossack who led a massive peasant revolt against Catherine, claiming to be the murdered Peter III. He was captured and publicly executed in Moscow.

✘ **All Poles** hated Catherine because she destroyed Poland as an independent state, making most of the country part of Russia.

What did Catherine do for Russia?

Above all, she made it bigger. The areas she took over included Crimea, Ukraine, Lithuania, Belarus, and most of Poland. But the majority of the Russian population remained peasant serfs — virtual slaves owned by landowners or by the state.

POTEMKIN VILLAGES

In 1787, **Prince Potemkin** organized a river trip through Russia for Catherine. To make the country look prosperous, he had fake villages built along the route. Like movie sets, they employed "extras" to act the part of jolly villagers, who waved as Catherine went by.

"Death is nothing, but to **live defeated**
. . . is to **die daily.**"

NAPOLEON
BONAPARTE

When I was twenty, the French overthrew their king in a revolution. I saw my chance to get involved and worked my way up the military ladder. Before long, I was the most popular general in France. Buoyed by my fame, I seized power and awarded myself an imperial crown.

Imperial Highs and Lows

As emperor, I humiliated the established rulers of Europe, beating them in battle after battle. At home, I gave the French order and discipline after the chaos of revolution. I invaded Russia with a great army but only a few ragged survivors returned. The rest froze to death as they retreated from Moscow. I despised the British as a nation of shopkeepers, yet their navy controlled the seas. In 1814, I was forced to surrender and was exiled to the island of Elba in the Mediterranean. But I wasn't finished yet.

I returned to France, where people flocked to welcome me. Marching at the head of another army, my magic failed me at Waterloo, and I suffered a crushing defeat. The British sent me to St. Helena, a remote island in the Atlantic Ocean, and this time there was no coming back.

TIMELINE

1769 Born in Ajaccio, Corsica, August 15

1798 Leads an army to Egypt

1804 Crowned emperor of France

1812 Failed invasion of Russia

1815 Final defeat at the Battle of Waterloo

1821 Dies a prisoner on St. Helena, May 5

WEIRD BUT TRUE

* As a child in Corsica, Napoleon spoke Italian. He always spoke French with an accent.

* Napoleon is often described as being short, but his 5-feet 6-inch (1.67-meter) stature was about average at that time.

* In France today, it is against the law for anyone to name a pig Napoleon.

LEGACY

Napoleon was a military genius who made himself emperor of France. He won control over most of Europe, but eventually the British defeated him. He created a code of law and a school system that still operate in France today.

BIG SPENDER

Born in Martinique in the Caribbean, **Joséphine de Beauharnais** (1763–1814) was Napoleon's first wife. She was a shopaholic, buying 900 dresses a year. When she failed to give Napoleon a son, he divorced her to marry Austrian Princess Marie-Louise in 1810.

ENEMIES

✘ **Horatio Nelson** (1758–1805) was the one-eyed, one-armed British admiral who defeated Napoleon's navy at the Battle of Trafalgar in 1805. The victory made Nelson a hero, but cost him his life.

✘ **The Duke of Wellington** (1769–1852) was the British general who took on Napoleon and beat him at the Battle of Waterloo.

?
Was Napoleon poisoned?
Napoleon's admirers believe that British guards on St. Helena deliberately poisoned him. It is also possible that he was poisoned accidentally, by arsenic used as a dye in the wallpaper of his room. A more likely story is that he died of stomach cancer.

"I have been chosen by fate to **break your chains.**"

SIMÓN BOLÍVAR

They call me "the Liberator." You'll see my statue wherever you go in South America — there I am, sword in hand, posing astride a horse. I'm revered as the hero who freed the South American colonies from Spanish rule. Sure, who doesn't love me now? If only it had been that way when I was alive.

So Near, Yet So Far

I was a genius at war. I fought in the swamps, the jungles, and the mountains, often with only a ragged band of followers. I knew we would never beat the Spanish without being as ruthless as they were. I made a Decree of War to the Death and, boy, did I mean it. My victorious invasion of Venezuela in 1813 was known as the Admirable Campaign.

Twelve years later, we'd driven the Spanish out of South America. Peru was the last to fall. I had visions of myself as president of a federation of all the freed states, bringing them liberty and justice. Instead, there were endless squabbles and fights. When I declared myself a dictator in an attempt to hold it all together, my enemies tried to kill me. That was about as much as I could take! I packed my bags for Europe, but died before I could leave.

TIMELINE

1783 Born in Caracas, Venezuela, July 24

1813 Leads an invasion of Venezuela

1821 President of the huge state of Gran Colombia

1825 Victory in independence war complete

1828 Declares himself dictator of Gran Colombia

1830 Dies at Santa Marta, Colombia, December 17

LEGACY

Bolívar led the long struggle to free South American colonies from Spanish rule. He wanted to be president of an independent South America. Though he drove the Spanish out, his dreams of presidency were never fulfilled.

WHAT'S IN A NAME?

* Bolívar's full name was Simón José Antonio de la Santísima Trinidad Bolívar y Palacios Ponte y Blanco.

* Bolívar is the only man to have two countries named after him — Bolivia and Venezuela (the Bolivarian Republic of Venezuela).

* Also named after Bolívar are an asteroid and a peninsula in Texas.

FRIENDS

+ **José de San Martín** (1778–1850) fought brilliant campaigns to free Argentina, Chile, and Peru from Spanish rule between 1812 and 1822.

+ **Manuela Sáenz** (1797–1856), Bolívar's mistress and close ally. After she helped him escape assassination in 1828, he called her "the Liberator's liberator."

? Was Bolívar murdered?

Bolívar died at 47. Many people said he was poisoned by political enemies, who had tried to assassinate him before. In 2011, his body was dug up and examined, but no evidence of poisoning was found. He probably died of tuberculosis.

GREAT LIBERATORS

★ **Toussaint l'Ouverture** (1743–1803) was a former slave who fought, successfully, to free Haiti from French rule.

★ **Fidel Castro** (b. 1926–) led a guerrilla campaign to take power from the American-backed, right-wing dicator, President Fulgencio Batista y Zaldívar in Cuba in 1959. Castro went on to rule until 2008.

"The prolonged **slavery of women** is the **darkest page** in human history."

ELIZABETH CADY
STANTON

Sometimes a single event can change your life forever. At the age of twenty-five, I married Henry Stanton, a man I admired for his radical views. For our honeymoon, he took me to an antislavery convention in London, England. I was filled with enthusiasm for the cause, but because I was a woman, I was not allowed to speak. Imagine that! The daughter of a privileged family, my father a congressman, and I lacked the most basic of human rights and freedoms. Worse still, even the most liberal-minded men couldn't see that the way they treated women was wrong. Well, I was not going to stand for that!

Fighting for Our Rights
In 1848, I organized a meeting on women's rights in my hometown of Seneca Falls, New York. We discussed many issues, with a focus on women's suffrage — the right to vote in elections.

I campaigned long and hard for the next half century. I never stopped believing that every citizen, regardless of race or gender, must have full voting rights. Sadly I died eighteen years before all women in the United States got the right to vote.

TIMELINE

1815 Born in Johnstown, New York, November 12

1840 Delegate to the World Antislavery Convention in London

1848 Organizes Women's Rights Convention at Seneca Falls

1869 National Woman Suffrage Association founded

1902 Dies in New York, October 26

SUFFRAGETTE SUCCESSES

* Wyoming gave women the vote in 1869, followed by Utah in 1870. Idaho and Colorado followed suit in the 1890s.

* The first country to give women full voting rights was New Zealand, in 1893.

* Passed in 1920, the Nineteenth Amendment guaranteed all American women the right to vote.

LEGACY
Elizabeth Cady Stanton was a founder of the American women's movement. She protested against the lowly position assigned to women in society and strove tirelessly to achieve equal rights.

IDA WELLS

Born in Mississippi in 1862, Ida Wells was an African–American woman who campaigned against racism and in favor of women's voting rights. She was especially famous for revealing the horrors of the lynching of black people in the southern United States. Wells died in 1931.

FRIENDS

+ **Lucretia Mott** (1793–1880) was a Quaker campaigner against slavery and for women's rights. She helped Stanton organize the Seneca Falls convention.

+ **Susan B. Anthony** (1820–1906) was cofounder with Stanton of the National Woman Suffrage Association. The two women also joined in protesting against alcohol abuse.

?
What was Stanton's attitude toward the church?
Stanton attacked the Christian church for teachings that encouraged women to be seen as second-class citizens. She described the Bible as one of the greatest obstacles to the liberation of women. Her views on religion were very controversial.

"**Workers** of the world **unite**;
you have nothing to lose but your **chains.**"

KARL MARX

I was a philosopher who wanted to change the world. Convinced that revolution was just around the corner, I devoted my life to overthrowing the society in which I lived. I joined a group called the Communist League and, with my friend Friedrich Engels, I wrote a Communist Manifesto to explain our revolutionary aims. Barely anyone read it!

Revolution Around the Corner
By sheer coincidence, people revolted against governments across Europe, and I was identified as a dangerous agitator. I took refuge in England, but London life was far from exciting. I was poor and had a family to support. We survived on money I earned writing articles for newspapers and on handouts from Engels. I spent most days in the Reading Room of the British Museum, researching and writing my heavyweight works. I wanted to prove that the revolution was definitely going to come one day.

My beard grew and so did my sorrows — when I died, I seemed to have achieved nothing. And, yet, a century later, large parts of the world had communist governments, which claimed to be ruling their countries according to my ideas!

TIMELINE

1818 Born in Trier, Germany, May 5

1848 Publishes **The Communist Manifesto**, cowritten with Friedrich Engels

1849 Settles in London

1864 Helps found the socialist First International

1867 Publishes first volume of his major work **Das Kapital**

1883 Dies in London, March 14

LEGACY
Karl Marx argued that the growth of an industrial society would inevitably lead to the workers revolting against their employers and taking control. His views later inspired communist revolutions in both Russia and China.

FRIEDRICH ENGELS
The son of a rich German businessman, Friedrich Engels (1820–1895) was Marx's closest collaborator. He became a revolutionary after witnessing the terrible conditions at one of his father's factories. Engels joined the family business and used the money to help Marx. Engels wrote his own books, which expanded on Marx's ideas.

KARL'S BIG IDEAS

* That history progressed in stages: First kings and nobles ran things, then bankers and businessmen took over, and in the future, workers would take control.

* That laws and governments always served the interests of the rich against the poor.

* That religion deliberately made people easy to govern.

?
Did Marx support the idea of a dictatorship?
Marx said that after the revolution there would be a "dictatorship of the proletariat." This meant that the working class (the proletariat) would hold all power. It did not mean a single individual would hold all power as a dictator.

FAST FACTS

* As a journalist, Marx contributed regularly to a US newspaper, the **New York Daily Tribune**.

* Marx believed that British prime minister Lord Palmerston was a secret Russian agent.

* Marx is buried in Highgate Cemetery, London. His tombstone reads: **"Workers of all lands unite."**

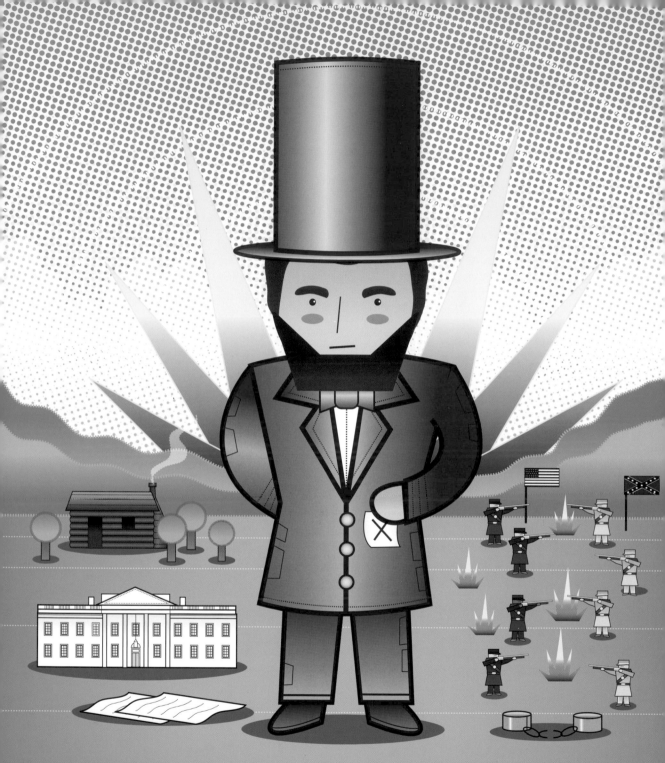

"As I would not be a **slave**, so I would not be a **master**. This expresses my idea of democracy."

ABRAHAM LINCOLN

I was born in a log cabin and I hated it — farm labor was not for me. So I taught myself to read and seized the chance America gave me to become a somebody — specifically, a small-time lawyer in Springfield, Illinois.

When I got involved in politics, people laughed at my lack of manners, but no one could deny my power as a speaker. The big issue of the day was slavery. I believed black people should be free to improve their lives by their own efforts just as I had. My views certainly caused a stir.

Civil War

I won the presidential election in 1860, but lost every slave-owning state of the South. Southern states began quitting the Union as soon as I hit the White House. I saw them as rebels who had to be fought to stop the breakup of the country I loved.

Plagued by backstabbing politicians and incompetent generals, I held the US government together through a civil war I'd never wanted. By the war's end, I had begun freeing slaves and guaranteeing black Americans the right to vote. But in my hour of victory, I was shot dead by a Southern fanatic.

TIMELINE

1809 Born in Kentucky, February 12

1830 Lincoln family moves to Illinois

1846 Elected to US House of Representatives

1860 Elected US president

1861 Civil War begins

1863 Emancipation Proclamation begins abolition of slavery

1864 Elected for a second presidential term

1865 Fatally shot by John Wilkes Booth, April 14

FAST FACTS

* At 6 feet 4 inches. (1 meter 93 centimeters), Abraham Lincoln is the tallest US president ever.

* Lincoln almost died at age nine when he got a concussion after being kicked in the head by a horse.

* Lincoln and his wife, Mary Todd Lincoln, had four sons. Only one lived to adulthood, the others died young of natural causes.

* Lincoln established Thanksgiving as an annual holiday in the United States, starting in November 1863.

LEGACY

The 16th president of the United States, Abraham Lincoln led the Union to victory in the Civil War. Known by many as the "Great Emancipator," Lincoln set his country on the path to the abolition of slavery with his promise of liberty for all.

FAVORITE GENERAL

Lincoln thought most of his generals in the Civil War were no good, but the exception was Ulysses S. Grant. Lincoln made Grant his commander-in-chief, saying, "I can't spare this man — he fights."

GETTYSBURG ADDRESS

Lincoln delivered his most famous speech on November 19, 1863, at the official opening of a soldiers' cemetery at Gettysburg, Pennsylvania. Lasting only a few minutes, the speech ended: ". . . Government of the people, by the people, for the people shall not perish from the earth."

? Who was Lincoln's assassin?

It was John Wilkes Booth, an actor and Confederate secret agent. At the time of the shooting, the president was sitting alongside his wife, watching a play at Ford's Theatre in Washington, D.C. Booth fled the scene, but was tracked down twelve days later and shot.

"**Knowledge** is the pathway from slavery to **freedom.**"

FREDERICK
DOUGLASS

I was born a slave in the southern United States. Bought and sold like a farm animal, I was mistreated and denied my freedom. Worse still, slave owners refused to accept that African–Americans could be smart — just imagine! Well, I learned to read and write, and taught other slaves, too. My rebellious streak didn't end there. At twenty, I fled to the northern states where an African–American could be free.

Freedom for All

Once I gained my freeedom, I joined the fight to end slavery throughout my country. Both white and black, we abolitionists were a small band but we sure made our voices heard. White people were amazed that I, a former slave, could speak so well. I went on to write my life story — a bestseller — and became famous, touring England and Ireland.

When the Civil War came in 1861, I wanted it to become a crusade to end slavery. President Lincoln was slow to see it that way, but I helped show him and other politicians that the time had come to outlaw slavery and give African–American people the vote. My efforts set the struggle against racial prejudice on the right path.

TIMELINE

1818 Born In Maryland, date unknown

1838 Escapes from slavery

1845 Publishes his life story

1847–1851 Runs **The North Star** newspaper

1861–1865 Advises President Lincoln during the Civil War

1895 Dies in Washington, D.C., February 20

LEGACY
Frederick Douglass campaigned for rights for all people, regardless of gender or race. His newspaper, **The North Star**, carried the slogan: "Right is of no sex — Truth is of no color   God is the father of us all, and we are all brethren."

VOTES FOR WOMEN

Douglass supported the call for women to have the right to vote and was the only African–American at the first women's rights convention in 1848. However, he refused to work for their cause jointly with his crusade to end slavery. He felt that combining forces would make both groups look weak.

FIGHTING SPIRIT

As punishment for teaching fellow slaves to read the Bible, Douglass was sent to work for Edward Covey, a farmer with a reputation for "breaking slaves." Douglass suffered multiple whippings and the ordeal almost broke him. One day he fought back, however. He humiliated Covey by beating him in a fistfight, after which Covey let him be. Douglass was just sixteen years old at the time.

?
How did Douglass manage to escape from slavery?
Aided by his soon-to-be wife, Douglass boarded a train in Maryland dressed as a sailor and carrying the ID papers of a free seaman. Within twenty-four hours, he was in a safe house in New York.

FRIENDS AND INFLUENCES

+ **William Lloyd Garrison** (1805–1879) Abolitionist and Douglass's mentor in his first years of freedom.

+ **Elizabeth Cady Stanton** (1815–1902) Early women's rights activist, who admired Douglass's support for votes for women.

+ **Abraham Lincoln** (1809–1865) US president who became a friend during the Civil War.

"We are **not interested** in the possibilities of **defeat**; they do **not exist!**"

QUEEN VICTORIA

When I became queen, the British monarchy seriously needed to clean up its act. The royal family was stuck in scandal, ridiculed in the press, and scorned by most of its subjects. Just eighteen at the time, I'd been raised in isolation in Kensington Palace and had no experience of the world.

Setting a Good Example
I married Albert, a German prince, and we dedicated ourselves to raising a family (and the tone of the country). We founded museums in London and created the Great Exhibition to show off the best of Britain. When Albert died of typhoid, I was crushed with grief. For thirteen years, I withdrew into mourning, refusing to attend any state occasions. People started to say that I should abdicate.

Reluctantly, I returned to my duties — after all, I was the head of an empire that spanned the globe. The British constitution kept me from wielding direct power, but I made my presence felt. This was an era of scientific and industrial advancement, with the British leading the way. By the end of my reign, Britain had become the most powerful country in the world.

TIMELINE

1819 Born in Kensington Palace, London, May 24

1837 Comes to the throne as Queen Victoria, at eighteen years of age

1840 Marries Prince Albert

1861 Prince Albert dies

1876 Accepts the title Empress of India

1901 Dies, January 22

FRIENDS

+ **Prince Albert of Saxe-Coburg and Gotha** (1819–1861), Victoria's beloved husband, was an intelligent man who promoted art and science.

+ **John Brown** (1826–1883), a Scottish servant, became the queen's closest companion following Albert's death.

+ **Benjamin Disraeli** (1804–1881), Victoria's favorite prime minister. He made her Empress of India.

LEGACY
A strong woman in a man's world, Victoria reigned for sixty-three years — longer than any other British monarch. She became a watchword for strict rules of conduct, setting the tone for the narrow-minded but clean-living Victorian era.

FAST FACTS

* Victoria survived two assassination attempts in which shots were fired, and five other physical assaults.

* Victoria had nine children and forty-two grandchildren.

* A conspiracy theory claims that Victoria's grandson, the Duke of Clarence (1864–92), was London's mysterious serial killer "Jack the Ripper."

A BRITISH SCANDAL

★ **King George IV** (1762–1830), Victoria's uncle, tried to divorce his wife and banned her from attending his coronation.

★ **King William IV** (1765–1837), another uncle, had ten children with his mistress but none with his wife.

★ **King Edward VII** (1841–1910), Victoria's son and successor, was a man who liked showgirls.

?
How many people did Victoria rule?
In 1900, Victoria reigned over more subjects than any other ruler on Earth. The British Empire contained about four hundred and twenty million people, almost a quarter of the entire world population at that time.

THE MODERN ERA

4

1879

BRIGHT SPARK

Thomas Edison lights up the United States with his incandescent lightbulb.

1847–1931
THOMAS EDISON

1898

RADIOACTIVE ELEMENT

Marie Curie announces her discovery of the chemical element radium.

1867–1934
MARIE CURIE

1905

SPACE AND TIME

Albert Einstein develops his special theory of relativity.

1879–1955
ALBERT EINSTEIN

1921

PEACEFUL PROTEST

The world watches as Gandhi takes on the British in India's bid for independence.

1869–1948
MOHANDAS GANDHI

1928

FATHER OF NATIONS

Joseph Stalin embarks on a reign of terror as dictator of the Soviet Union.

1878–1953
JOSEPH STALIN

One great inventor, two scientists, and three dictators stand among the men and women who made history from the late 1800s to the present day. Among them are archenemies Hitler and Churchill, and three of the greatest freedom fighters of all time: Mohandas Gandhi, Martin Luther King Jr., and Nelson Mandela. Between them, they sum up the highs and lows of this modern era — not just a time of discovery, but also of war and upheaval.

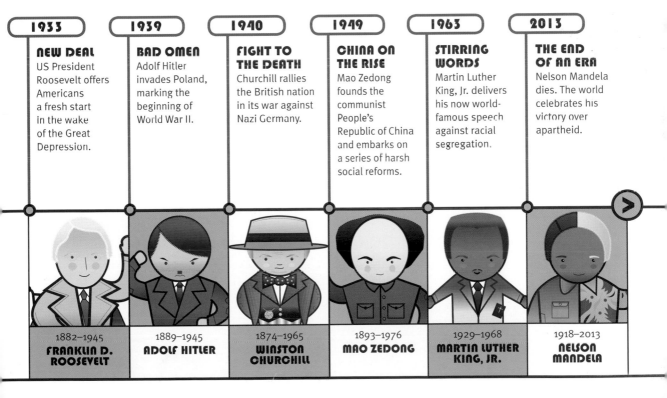

1933

NEW DEAL
US President Roosevelt offers Americans a fresh start in the wake of the Great Depression.

1939

BAD OMEN
Adolf Hitler invades Poland, marking the beginning of World War II.

1940

FIGHT TO THE DEATH
Churchill rallies the British nation in its war against Nazi Germany.

1949

CHINA ON THE RISE
Mao Zedong founds the communist People's Republic of China and embarks on a series of harsh social reforms.

1963

STIRRING WORDS
Martin Luther King, Jr. delivers his now world-famous speech against racial segregation.

2013

THE END OF AN ERA
Nelson Mandela dies. The world celebrates his victory over apartheid.

1882–1945
FRANKLIN D. ROOSEVELT

1889–1945
ADOLF HITLER

1874–1965
WINSTON CHURCHILL

1893–1976
MAO ZEDONG

1929–1968
MARTIN LUTHER KING, JR.

1918–2013
NELSON MANDELA

"Genius is one percent **inspiration,**
ninety-nine percent **perspiration.**"

THOMAS EDISON

A true American hero, I worked my way up from rock bottom to the very top. I started working at just twelve years old. I sold newspapers and candy to railroad passengers.

The Wizard of Menlo Park

My big break came with a job operating the electric telegraph. Zipping Morse code messages along a wire was cutting-edge technology in the 1860s! I came up with some improvements to the telegraph and realized there was money to be made out of marketing new gadgets. I put a whole team to work in a research laboratory at Menlo Park, New Jersey. I wasn't first with the telephone — that honor went to Alexander Graham Bell — but my phonograph was a sensation. Who would have believed sound could be recorded and played back?

My next idea was another doozie: the electric lightbulb. The ideas kept on coming and, make no mistake, selling was just as important to me as inventing. By the time I died, I held a record 1,093 US patents (documents stating that only I could make the products they listed). I had changed how people lived — and I'd made a ton of money besides.

TIMELINE

1847 Born in Milan, Ohio, February 11

1867 Starts experimenting with the telegraph

1869 Becomes a full-time inventor and businessman

1876 Establishes a laboratory at Menlo Park

1879 Invents the incandescent lightbulb

1931 Dies in New Jersey, October 18

LEGACY

Thomas Edison was a leading light in the Age of Invention, when ingenious new gadgets transformed everyday life. A good businessman, not only did he develop new technologies but he turned them into instant mass-market products.

THAT LIGHTBULB MOMENT

Edison was not the first scientist to create light using electricity, but he did discover how to make electric light last longer. When an electric current passes through a very fine wire, called a filament, the wire gets so hot that it glows (making it incandescent). Edison experimented with thousands of materials for the filament, until he discovered that carbon could glow for days without burning up.

FIRST AND LAST

* Edison's first patent was for an electronic vote recorder.
* The first recording on the phonograph was of Edison reading **Mary Had a Little Lamb**.
* Edison's last breath, exhaled on his deathbed, was captured in a test tube and is now in the **Henry Ford Museum** in Dearborn, Michigan.

?

Did Edison invent the movies?
Not quite. Although Edison's kinetoscope showed moving images, they could only be viewed by one person at a time. The first people to project a movie on a screen in a theater were French brothers, Auguste and Louis Lumière, in 1895.

EDISON'S INVENTIONS

* The phonograph, recording sound on a cylinder (1877).
* The incandescent lightbulb (1879).
* Power stations for generating electricity (1882).
* The kinetoscope, an early motion-picture device and a forerunner of the movies (1894).
* Alkaline storage batteries for use in early electric cars (1901).

"Nothing in life is to be **feared**,
it is only to be **understood**."

MARIE CURIE

I'm famous as one of the world's greatest scientists, but success didn't come easy. I started out as Marie Sklodowska in Poland, where life was tough for girls. People didn't expect us to study science and we certainly couldn't go to a university. I was desperate to learn and left for France. In Paris I was allowed to study at the Sorbonne University, where I met my husband, Pierre Curie, who was as passionate about science as I was.

With only a leaky shed for a lab, we worked day and night. We were trying to understand the strange radiation that I had dubbed "radioactivity." We weren't afraid of the stuff, even though it made our hands glow in the dark. Eventually, we found tiny amounts of two radioactive elements no one had ever seen before. We called them polonium and radium.

World Recognition
Pierre died in a car accident in 1906, and I had to continue our work alone. I faced prejudice in France — both as a foreigner and as a woman — but I overcame it all. I went on to become the first female professor at the Sorbonne and won renown across the globe.

TIMELINE

1867 Born in Poland, November 7

1895 Marries Professor Pierre Curie in Paris

1898 Announces the discovery of radium and polonium

1903 Wins her first Nobel Prize

1911 Wins her second Nobel Prize

1934 Dies in France, July 4

RADIUM TOOTHPASTE
When Marie Curie first discovered radium, manufacturers used it to make clocks and watches glow in the dark. Scientists even marketed it as a health product, adding it to toothpaste. The truth about the dangers of radiation emerged very slowly. Today, anyone handling radium must wear protective clothing so that it does not harm them.

LEGACY
Marie Curie discovered the radioactive element radium, which lay hidden in tiny amounts in other minerals. Curie wanted her discoveries to do good in the world, and believed radium could cure disease, especially cancer.

FRIENDS
+ **Pierre Curie** (1859–1906) was Marie's husband and scientific collaborator.
+ **Henri Becquerel** (1852–1908) was the French physicist who first discovered radiation in uranium. His work inspired the Curies and he shared the Nobel Prize with them in 1903.

RECORD BREAKER
Marie Curie was the first woman to win a **Nobel Prize**, sharing the prize for physics in 1903. Eight years later she was awarded the prize for chemistry. At the time, she was the first person to have won more than one Nobel Prize. Today, she is still the only woman ever to have won the prize more than once.

?
Did Curie die of radiation?
Marie Curie used to carry radioactive radium around in her pockets. She had no idea radiation was harmful. She went almost blind with cataracts on her eyes and died of bone cancer — both almost certainly caused by exposure to radiation.

"**Imagination** is more
important than knowledge."

ALBERT EINSTEIN

With hair as wild as my ideas, I'm the superstar scientist who took the world by storm. My buzzword was "relativity." In the universe I described, nothing was fixed — not even time and space — everything depended on your point of view. I began publishing my theories in 1905. Back then, I was a nobody in Switzerland with an office job and a passion for physics. Fourteen years later, however, astronomers observing an eclipse of the sun proved my theories were right. Suddenly, I became one of the most famous people on the planet. Of course, you would have to be a physicist to understand what my theories meant, but I can tell you they changed the world.

Explosive Equation

I was also famous for an equation: $E = mc^2$. This tricky little formula made a big impact, because other scientists showed how it could help make nuclear weapons. I was sorry to see my work put to such destructive uses. In my old age, I campaigned for a world government to abolish war. I also searched for a single "unified theory" to explain how all the forces in the universe worked — but I never found it.

TIMELINE

1879 Born in Germany, March 14

1905 Publishes the special theory of relativity

1921 Wins the Nobel Prize

1933 Moves to the United States

1939 Warns that Germany is building a nuclear bomb

1955 Dies in America, April 18

LEGACY

Einstein's equation $E = mc^2$ says that energy (E) is equal to mass (m) times the speed of light (c) squared. It shows that even the tiniest particle of matter is able to release a huge amount of energy. It paved the way for the creation of the atom bomb.

ESCAPING DEATH

Albert Einstein was Jewish. In 1933, the Nazis came to power in Germany and began persecuting Jews. Einstein was forced to flee to the United States. Later, the Nazis tried to kill all Jews in the Holocaust. Escaping to America had saved Einstein's life. He helped save other Jews from the Nazis, too.

EINSTEIN'S BRAIN

When Einstein died, in 1955, his brain was removed from his body and preserved. (He may not have agreed to this when he was alive.) Scientists studied it to see what it was that made him such a genius. But they discovered that his brain was not out of the ordinary after all.

?

Is it true that Einstein failed to get good grades at school?
Not entirely! Einstein was a late developer and slow to learn to speak. At school he wasn't obviously bright, but he always got good grades in a few subjects, especially math. He did well enough in the end to get into university.

THREE BIG IDEAS

✳ That a person will age more slowly the faster he or she travels (his idea being that time passes more slowly with speed).

✳ That light travels in packets of energy.

✳ That gravity bends light — and that this is the effect that creates "black holes" in space.

"My life is my message."

MOHANDAS GANDHI

My home country, India, was known as the jewel in the British crown, but the Indian people wanted freedom from British rule. I taught them to fight for independence — not with weapons, but with nonviolent disobedience. I believed that if they could accept beatings with sticks and not hit back, their oppressors would feel ashamed of their actions and stop. Leading by example, I dressed like one of the Indian poor. I broke British laws and was sent to prison more times than I could count. I went on hunger strikes that brought me to the brink of death. My admirers called me Mahatma (Great Soul).

Toward a New Peace
The British invited me to a conference in London, in 1931, but progress was slow. I spent many more years in prison before India finally became independent in 1947. Even then my dream was unfulfilled. I had wanted India to be a place where people of all religions could live in harmony, but Muslim Pakistan was split from the rest of the country. I struggled to make peace between Muslims and Hindus — and, for my efforts, I was shot dead by one of my own countrymen.

TIMELINE

1869 Born in Gujarat, India, October 2

1894 Begins work as a lawyer in South Africa

1914 Moves to India, where he campaigns against British rule

1921 Becomes leader of the Indian independence movement

1930 Leads the famous Salt March in protest at British policies

1948 Assassinated by a Hindu extremist in New Delhi, January 30

GANDHI IN SOUTH AFRICA

Gandhi first became a political campaigner as a lawyer in South Africa. He was outraged by racism that, for example, forced an Asian to give up a seat on a train to a white person. Gandhi learned about the power of civil disobedience while organizing protests against racial laws in South Africa.

LEGACY

Gandhi built a mass movement based on civil disobedience (nonviolent resistance to unjust laws). His campaign against British rule in India was later an inspiration to American Martin Luther King Jr. and the civil rights movement.

BIG IDEAS

* Gandhi rejected Western consumerism and industry, wanting people to live a simple life instead.

* He called his nonviolent passive resistance **Satyagraha**, which means "the force of truth."

* He protested against the caste (class) system that existed in India, which made the poorest people despised as untouchables.

ASSASSINATION

In 1948, Gandhi was working tirelessly for peace between Hindus and Muslims in India and Pakistan. Some Indian Hindus saw Gandhi as pro-Muslim and a traitor to their cause. On January 30, Hindu extremist Nathuram Godse shot Gandhi dead during a public prayer meeting held at his home in New Delhi.

? What was the Salt March?

A particularly unpopular aspect of British rule in India was a tax imposed on salt. In 1930, Gandhi led a march to the sea, to take free salt from the water illegally. The march focused the world's attention on his cause.

"I **trust no one**, not even **myself**."

JOSEPH STALIN

Stalin means "Man of Steel" — I like the sound of that! I was in Russia in 1917 when Communist Party leader Vladimir Lenin seized power and set up the first communist state. As secretary for the Communist Party, I kept a low profile, so people didn't notice how cunning I was. When Lenin died, I outwitted all my rivals to make myself dictator.

Reign of Terror
Racked by paranoia, I used my secret police to eliminate all possible rivals. They arrested, tortured, and executed thousands of party members and government officials in what became known as the Great Purge. I forced peasants into collective farms at gunpoint. Millions starved in famines or died in prison camps. I made a pact with Hitler in 1939, but he invaded Russia two years later. There was no way I'd let him destroy my country so I fought back. I defeated his army and captured Berlin.

After the war, I forced communist dictatorship on the countries I had conquered and developed an atom bomb to match America's. Millions were still held in prison camps, but I had made the Soviet Union into one of the world's two superpowers.

TIMELINE

1878 Born in Gori, Georgia, a part of Russia, December 18

1917 Takes part in the Russian Revolution

1928 Established as undisputed leader of the Soviet Union

1936 Launches the Great Purge; hundreds of thousands are executed

1945 His Red Army occupies Eastern Europe

1953 Dies in Moscow, March 5

LEGACY
Stalin ruled the former Russian Empire with an iron fist. He transformed the communist Soviet Union into an industrial and military giant, but at the cost of millions of lives. In World War II, he joined Britain and the United States in defeating Hitler.

FAST FACTS

✳ Stalin's original name was **Josef Vissarionovich Dzhugashvili**.

✳ Before he became a revolutionary, Stalin was a theology student, training to become a priest in the Orthodox Church.

✳ Stalin's face was scarred by smallpox. When a portrait painter showed him as he really was, Stalin had the artist killed.

COMMUNIST THEORY

Under the communist system a single political party holds all power. It controls the government, the economy, and every aspect of society. Communism was supposed to create equality and to free working people from exploitation by the rich. In practice, it often led to oppression by secret police and a denial of freedom.

How many people suffered under Stalin?
Some claim that Stalin was responsible for at least twenty million deaths. Most were not massacred directly on his orders, but died through hardship, hunger, or ill treatment, resulting from his policies.

RIVALS

✗ **Vladimir Lenin** (1870–1924) was the first leader of the Soviet Union. Before his death, he warned against Stalin's growing power.

✗ Stalin defeated **Leon Trotsky** (1879–1940) in the power struggle that followed Lenin's death. Stalin drove Trotsky into exile and eventually ordered his assassination in Mexico.

"The **only** thing we have to fear is **fear itself**."

FRANKLIN D. ROOSEVELT

Picture the United States in the grip of the Great Depression. The homeless live in shacks and people have to wait in line for loaves of bread. Who would you turn to as your savior? Well, the American people turned to me, FDR, son of one of the richest families in New York State. I didn't disappoint them, either. By the end of my first one hundred days as president, I had given America fresh hope with a set of laws and social programs called the New Deal.

America's Hero

Of course, I couldn't solve all of our country's problems, but I did provide many people with work and I got the country moving forward again. Millions listened to my fireside chats on the radio and felt they had a true friend in the White House. They voted for me again and again and again — I served four terms!

Eventually, the American people followed me into World War II against Germany and Japan. I wanted victory in the war to create a future world that was free from fear and violence. Sadly, I never lived to see whether my dream came true. I died less than a month before the Allied forces defeated Hitler.

TIMELINE

1882 Born at Hyde Park, New York, January 30

1905 Marries Eleanor Roosevelt, a distant cousin

1921 Partially paralyzed after contracting polio

1933 Becomes US president and launches the New Deal

1941 Leads the United States into World War II

1945 Dies at his retreat, Little White House, in Warm Springs, Georgia, April 12

ELECTION FACTS

✳ Roosevelt won four presidential elections in a row.

✳ He is the only American president to have served more than two terms in the White House.

✳ Each time Roosevelt was sworn in as president, he took the oath on an old family Bible, which was written in Dutch.

✳ He died three months after being inaugurated for his fourth term.

LEGACY

The cousin of an earlier president (Teddy Roosevelt), FDR was the 32nd president of the United States. Occupying the White House for twelve years, he led the United States through the Great Depression and into World War II.

FIRST LADY

Eleanor Roosevelt, FDR's wife, was a political activist with her own reform agenda. She was a leading campaigner for civil rights and rights for women. Often more radical than her husband, she sometimes disagreed with his policies.

SURVIVING THE GUN

Roosevelt almost failed to reach the White House. In January 1933, before his first inauguration, he survived an assassination attempt. His would-be assassin fired five gunshots in total. All of them missed Roosevelt, but one hit — and killed — the mayor of Chicago, who was sitting alongside him.

? Was FDR paralyzed?

Yes. When in his thirties, Roosevelt became paralyzed from the waist down after getting polio. He spent much of his time in a wheelchair, but took pains to appear on his own two feet in public. Few Americans knew the truth about his paralysis at the time.

"He who would **live**, must **fight**."

ADOLF HITLER

As I saw it, war was good, because only the toughest survived. During World War I, I fought for four years in the German army, and was gassed and shelled. When Germany lost the war, I was out for revenge and looking for someone to blame.

Dictatorship and War

I held strongly racist opinions. I claimed the Jews were plotting against Germany in a worldwide conspiracy. I led the National Socialist (Nazi) Party, campaigning to rebuild Germany after the defeat of World War I and to overpower the Jews. I stirred up my followers with my violent speeches and had my Stormtroopers beat up my enemies. Becoming head of the government in 1933, I soon took total power, shutting anyone I didn't like away in work camps called concentration camps.

I built up the German military forces, took over Austria, and destroyed Czechoslovakia. World War II started when I invaded Poland. I was unbeatable — by 1941, I ruled most of Europe. Life was hell for those I conquered. But the Allies were too strong and the tide of war turned. As my enemies overran Germany, I killed myself in my bunker in Berlin.

TIMELINE

1889 Born in Austria on April 20

1914–1918 Serves in German army in World War I

1933 Becomes German chancellor

1935 Declared Führer of the Third Reich

1939 Invades Poland, starting World War II

1945 Commits suicide in Berlin, April 30

LEGACY

Adolf Hitler was a racist and a mass murderer. As dictator of Germany he was guilty of many crimes. His actions led to World War II, in which 70 million people died worldwide. He lost the war to the Allies in 1945.

CRIMES AGAINST HUMANITY

✳ Around six million Jews were killed in what is now known as the Holocaust.

✳ One in six of the murdered Jews died at Auschwitz concentration camp.

✳ Auschwitz and several other sites were used as work camps, but also for killing the millions of people that Hitler targeted.

RIVAL POWERS

✳ In 1939, the **Allied forces** fighting against Germany were Britain, France, and Poland. They were joined by many other countries as the war raged, most notably Russia and the United States.

✳ Hitler's Germany was joined by Italy and Japan in its fight against the Allies. Together, they were known as the **Axis Powers**.

?

Why did Hitler target the Jews?
Hitler's goal was the triumph of a German master race. He saw the Jews (and many other races) as inferior. The Nazis killed millions of Jews, Poles, and Russians as well as hundreds of thousands of socialists, communists, gay people, and disabled people.

FELLOW DICTATORS

★ **Benito Mussolini** (1883–1945) made himself dictator of Italy as leader of the Fascist Party. He became Hitler's closest ally.

★ **General Francisco Franco** (1892–1975) became dictator of Spain with the help of Hitler and Mussolini. They sent troops and aircraft to help Franco win the Spanish Civil War (1936–1939).

"We shall NEVER surrender."

WINSTON CHURCHILL

My life was one of nonstop adventure. As a young man, I fought in the wars of the British Empire. I rode in a cavalry charge in the Sudan and escaped from a Boer prisoner-of-war camp in South Africa. Then I became a politician and a top government minister while still in my thirties. Well, it was all too good to last. . . .

From Zero to Hero

After Britain entered World War I, I had a brilliant idea to send troops to a place called Gallipoli in Turkey. It was a disaster and I was disgraced. In the 1930s, I warned that Britain needed to prepare to fight Nazi Germany, but no one listened. By spring 1940, Britain stood alone against the Nazi invasion. Appointed prime minister, I declared a fight to the death.

My defiant radio speeches rank among the greatest ever. I was ready to do anything for victory — even partner with communist Russia. My wartime meetings with the Soviet dictator, Stalin, and President Roosevelt shaped the postwar world. I was shocked when the British people voted me out of office at the war's end. I had led the country to victory, after all!

TIMELINE

1874 Born at Blenheim Palace, Oxfordshire, November 30

1895–1900 Serves as an army officer

1900 Elected to parliament

1908 Becomes a government minister

1915 Blamed for military disaster at Gallipoli in modern-day Turkey

1940–1945 Serves as British prime minister in World War II

1965 Dies in London, January 24

AMERICAN HERITAGE

Winston Churchill was half-American. His mother, Jennie Jerome, was the daughter of an American millionaire. Tracing his family tree, researchers have found links to both George Washington and the presidential Bush family. In 1963, Winston Churchill became the first person to be made an honorary citizen of the United States.

LEGACY

Sir Winston Churchill was a resolute prime minister who led Britain to victory in World War II. He took power during the country's "darkest hour," inspiring the British people with his refusal to give in to the Germans.

AS WELL AS WINNING THE WAR . . .

* Churchill was an aviation pioneer. He learned to fly and created the Royal Navy Air Service, in 1912.

* He pushed for the development of the first tanks during World War I.

* He won the Nobel Prize in Literature in 1953, for books he wrote on history and his biographies.

FAST FACTS

* Churchill hated school and got very poor grades.

* He began smoking cigars when visiting Cuba, aged twenty-one. He kept a store of several thousand cigars in his home.

* He took up painting as a hobby. Churchill's landscapes now sell at auction for around one million dollars each.

?

Is it true that Churchill held meetings while in bed?
Churchill sometimes invited his chief military advisers to talk to him in his bedroom. He adopted the habit of taking a siesta, after discovering the custom while fighting for the Spanish in Cuba (1895).

"Political power grows out of the barrel of a gun."

MAO ZEDONG

When I grew up, China was in chaos. Change had to happen, even if it cost millions of lives. That's the way I saw it, anyway. My communist pals and I became guerrilla fighters. In 1934, I led a Long March, across 8,000 miles (12,800 km) of tough country, to escape massacre by the Chinese Nationalists. We built up our strength and finally, in 1949, drove the nationalists out of the country.

A Fresh Start

Taking power was just the beginning. I wanted to destroy the old China and build a new one.

I thought I could inspire the nation with revolutionary slogans. In 1958, I declared a Great Leap Forward, abolishing private enterprise and forcing everyone to live in communes. A huge dive in output and mass starvation followed, but that didn't stop me.

In 1966, I declared a Cultural Revolution, seeking to wipe out traditional ideas and replace them with my theories. This was another disaster, causing many more deaths. Yet my efforts also made China strong. In 1972, President Richard Nixon came to meet with me. After he left, he accepted that the China I had built was a power to be reckoned with.

TIMELINE

1893 Born in Hunan province, China, December 26

1921 Founding member of the Chinese Communist Party

1949 Founds the People's Republic of China

1958 The Great Leap Forward causes mass starvation

1966 Launches the Cultural Revolution

1976 Dies in Beijing, September 9

LEGACY

Mao Zedong was the first leader of communist China. He came to power following a guerrilla war lasting twenty years. Once in control, his drive to revolutionize Chinese society caused death and upheaval on an enormous scale.

GUERRILLAS

Mao has been credited with the invention of revolutionary guerrilla warfare, which uses lightly armed fighters, who are based, initially, in remote forests or mountains. They gather support from the rural population, who then help them fight their way to power. Fidel Castro in Cuba and Ho Chi Minh in Vietnam are among other leaders who imitated the idea.

CULTURAL REVOLUTION

The **Cultural Revolution** was mostly an attack on China's educated elite. Young people, known as Red Guards, staged mass demonstrations waving the **Little Red Book**. They publicly humiliated people they considered elite — like teachers — and forced them to do manual work in factories.

?
What was the Little Red Book?

It was a collection of Mao's thoughts and quotes, officially known as **Quotations from Chairman Mao Zedong**. It had a bright red cover, hence the nickname. It is one of the most published books of all time.

FAST FACTS

✳ As a student in 1915, Mao wrote the longest-ever recorded graffiti — four thousand Chinese characters criticizing the school system.

✳ Mao married four times. His fourth wife, Jiang Qing, was a famous movie star before she married him.

✳ In 1966, at the age of seventy, Mao led a mass swim in the Yangtze River.

"Life's most persistent and urgent question is, 'What are you doing for others?'"

MARTIN LUTHER KING, JR.

As a young Baptist minister in the South, in the 1950s, I could not close my eyes to the prejudice against African–Americans. Driven by a love of justice, I became a leader of the civil rights movement. This nonviolent movement sought equal treatment for African–Americans. But my efforts were met with violence. My home was bombed, I was arrested (twenty-nine times!), I marched under showers of bricks and bottles. It was hard to endure without hitting back, but I knew that if I stood up for what was right, justice would be on my side.

Fighting Prejudice

My powerful speeches inspired a campaign that made the US government pass laws against discrimination. These laws forced many white people to face up to their prejudices. Many people rejected my views — not only white racists but also young black people who wanted to meet violence with violence.

When I protested against poverty, I was denounced as a communist. When I attacked America's war in Vietnam, I was described as unpatriotic. But I kept to my course. In the end, an enemy's bullet silenced me.

TIMELINE

1929 Born in Atlanta, Georgia, January 15

1953 Marries Coretta Scott

1955 Leads a bus boycott in Birmingham, Alabama

1963 Heads the March on Washington

1964 Awarded the Nobel Peace Prize

1968 Assassinated in Memphis, Tennessee, April 4

"I HAVE A DREAM"

King's most famous speech was made at the end of the March on Washington in August 1963. It expressed his dream that, in the future, Americans would "not be judged by the color of their skin but by the content of their character."

LEGACY

Martin Luther King Jr. led a nonviolent campaign against racial segregation and in favor of equal rights for African–Americans. His work had a huge influence on the civil rights movement, and he received the Nobel Peace Prize for his efforts.

FRIEND OR FOE?

✘ **J. Edgar Hoover** (1895–1972), head of the FBI, regarded King as dangerous. He recorded King's phone calls, bugged his hotel rooms, and even tried to blackmail him.

✘ **Malcolm X** (1925–1965), an African–American Muslim activist. He believed in the same cause, yet rejected King's nonviolent approach to fighting racism. He, too, was assassinated.

ASSASSINATION

On April 4, 1968, Martin Luther King, Jr. was shot dead while standing on a balcony at the Lorraine Motel in Memphis, Tennessee. Following a manhunt lasting two months, an escaped convict, James Earl Ray, was convicted of the killing. Today, some people question his guilt.

?

Who was King's hero?
Martin Luther King, Jr. was inspired by the example of Indian nationalist Mohandas Gandhi. He adopted Gandhi's idea of civil disobedience, refusing to obey unjust laws and meeting violence with peaceful resistance.

"There is **no easy walk** to freedom."

NELSON MANDELA

A true optimist, I believed that love came more naturally than hate. But I was also a black man in white-ruled South Africa, where the government imposed a system of racial segregation, called apartheid. From an early age, I dedicated my life to ending this injustice. I joined the African National Congress (ANC), organizing peaceful protests against a regime that responded with brutal violence.

From Prisoner to President

In 1960, government forces fired on demonstrators at Sharpeville. I saw that the regime could only be overthrown by force and began to organize armed resistance. I was captured by the police and sent to prison. I spent eighteen years in a cell on Robben Island and almost another decade in other prisons.

Life was tough, but I never lost faith. When the white government finally decided to talk to me, I insisted on a complete end to apartheid. In 1994, I was elected president of South Africa. I pursued peace and reconciliation, so that my country would never again be a place of hatred and oppression. When I died, in 2013, I was celebrated around the world as one of the greatest men who had ever lived.

TIMELINE

1918 Born in Cape Province, South Africa, July 18

1942 Joins African National Congress

1962 Arrested and imprisoned

1990 Released for negotiations with the white government

1994 Elected president of South Africa

1999 Retires from the presidency

2013 Dies, Johannesburg, South Africa, December 5

LEGACY

Nelson Mandela was the first black president of South Africa. He brought an end to apartheid and introduced an era of racial tolerance in South Africa. He established full civil rights for all in a "Rainbow Nation."

ALLIES

+ **President F. W. de Klerk** (b. 1936) was leader of the pro-apartheid National Party. In 1990, he negotiated with Mandela to end apartheid, and he later served as vice president in Mandela's government.

+ **Bishop Desmond Tutu** (b. 1931) headed the Truth and Reconciliation Commission, set up by Mandela to investigate crimes of the apartheid era.

APARTHEID

Under South Africa's apartheid system, different races were segregated by color and Africans, in particular, were subjected to gross oppression. They could not move freely around the country, had little access to education, and were not permitted to vote or own land.

? Did Mandela use violence?

At first, Mandela followed the path of nonviolent civil disobedience, but the brutal response of the white regime convinced him otherwise. He embarked on an armed struggle, with his organization carrying out bombings and other acts of sabotage.

FAST FACTS

✳ Mandela was originally named **Rolihlahla**, which means "troublemaker." He took the name Nelson when he went to school.

✳ He trained as a lawyer and opened the first black law practice in South Africa.

✳ Mandela was awarded the Nobel Peace Prize jointly with F. W. de Klerk in 1993.

GLOSSARY

AGITATOR A person who encourages other people to protest or rebel against the government ruling their country.

ALLIANCE An agreement between different countries or political groups to act together — for example, in fighting a war against a common enemy.

ALLY A member of an alliance. In World War II the countries fighting against Nazi Germany, Italy, and Japan were known as "the Allies."

ATOM The tiniest part of an element that has all the properties of that element. A source of energy in nuclear power stations, atoms are also the explosive force in atom bombs.

BOTANY The scientific study of plants.

CATHOLIC A Christian who belongs to the Roman Catholic Church. The Roman Catholic Church is under the leadership of the Pope.

COLONIZE To send people from your own country to settle in, and take control of, another land.

CONQUEST The act of taking control of another country or people by armed force.

CONVERT To adopt a different religious faith or set of beliefs.

CRUCIFY To kill a person by attaching them to a wooden cross. As a form of execution, it was used frequently by the ancient Romans.

CULT An extremist group, usually centered around a single powerful individual. Cults often follow beliefs and practices that are at odds with the rest of society.

DICTATOR A leader who exercises absolute power. Dictators rule without regard for law or individual freedom.

DIPLOMAT A person who represents his or her country abroad. Diplomats handle relations with foreign governments and officials.

DYNASTY A series of rulers of a country — monarchs or emperors — who all belong to the same family by birth or adoption.

ENLIGHTENMENT The Enlightenment was a movement of thinkers in eighteenth-century Europe and North America. Followers believed in individual human rights and used reason to challenge traditional beliefs and authority.

EXILE Being banned from living in your native country, usually for political reasons.

GEOLOGY The scientific study of the earth, including rocks, earthquakes, and volcanoes.

GEOMETRY The branch of math that deals with lines and shapes — for example, triangles, squares, and cubes.

HEATHEN A person regarded as having no religious beliefs.

HERESY Having an opinion, theory, or belief that disagrees with the accepted theories and beliefs of a major religious group, especially among Christians.

HOLOCAUST Mass slaughter. This term is used to refer to the mass murder of Jews by the Nazis in Europe during World War II.

ILLEGITIMATE Refers to a person whose parents were not married at the time of his or her birth.

IMMORTAL Living forever.

LEGACY Something handed down from one generation to the next, be it property and money or ideas and achievements.

LYNCH When a mob of people attacks and kills a person for a crime he or she is supposed to have committed, but without giving the accused a trial of any kind.

MARAUD To go around a place causing trouble, often by attacking people and property.

MARTYR A person who is prepared to suffer, and even die, rather than give up his or her beliefs.

MAUSOLEUM A large building constructed to contain the tombs of important people such as emperors.

METEOROLOGY The scientific study of the weather.

MUMMIFY To preserve a dead body by embalming it and wrapping it in cloth. This technique was often used in ancient Egypt.

MUSLIM A believer in Islam, a religious faith founded in the seventh century CE. The faith was founded by the Prophet Muhammad in the modern-day Middle East.

MUTINY A rebellion against authority, especially by soldiers or sailors against their officers. Mutineers typically refuse to obey orders from their superiors.

NUCLEAR RADIATION This term refers to minute particles or rays given off naturally by certain substances. Such particles are also produced in nuclear explosions. Exposure to some forms of radiation can be harmful to the body.

PAGAN This term is used for people who do not belong to any of the major world religions, such as Christianity, Judaism, and Islam.

PATENT An official license (a type of document) making an inventor the only person who can use his or her invention during a certain period of time. Anybody else wanting to use the invention must pay the inventor to do so.

PATRIOT A person who loves his or her own country and stands up for it against its enemies.

PERSECUTE To ill-treat a person, or a group of people, unjustly because of their race or gender or for their religious or political beliefs.

PHILOSOPHER A person who thinks about fundamental questions such as the meaning of life, the basis of our understanding of the universe, and the nature of good and evil.

PLANETARIUM A building in which images of stars and planets are projected onto a dome. The images are used to educate and entertain an audience.

PREJUDICE To have a negative opinion of a person or a group of people, where the opinion is formed without any consideration of fact, evidence, or rational argument.

PROTESTANT A member of various Christian churches that reject the authority of the Catholic Pope. These Protestant churches include Baptists, Anglicans, Lutherans, Presbyterians, Methodists, and Quakers, among others.

PSYCHOLOGY The scientific study of the human mind and of human behavior.

RACISM The belief that some races are naturally superior to others. Racists believe they have the right to dominate and discriminate against other races.

RADICAL In politics, a radical is a person who wants fundamental change in the way society or government is organized.

SACK To lay waste to a town or city, destroying buildings, stealing property, and killing or seriously harming the inhabitants. In medieval times a city was usually sacked after a successful siege.

SIEGE The surrounding of a defended city or fortress by a hostile army. The purpose is to cut the city off from supplies from outside.

TREATY A written agreement between two countries. Wars often end with a peace treaty between the opposing states.

WOMEN'S SUFFRAGE "Suffrage" means the right to vote in political elections. The campaign for women's suffrage demanded that women be given the right to vote on the same basis as men.

ZOOLOGY The scientific study of all aspects of animal life.

INDEX